라이언 쌤,
이렇게 가르쳐서

영어수업
대박내다
Ⅱ

지은이 **박용호**

본명보다 '라이언 쌤'으로 더 알려진 대한민국 영어교사. 딱딱하고 지루한 수업 방식에서 벗어나 학생들의 영어 귀와 입을 뜨게 하는 재미있는 수업으로 학생들의 사랑을 받고 있다. '제 2회 전국 중등영어교사 수업 경진대회'에서 대상을 수상한 후 독창적인 그의 수업 방법이 MBC, KBS 등의 각종 프로그램과 신문, 잡지 등에 소개되면서 세간의 주목을 받고 있다. 2007년부터 강원도부터 제주도까지 전국의 모든 영어 교사들에게 자신의 뻔뻔(fun fun)한 수업 비법을 전수하는 '교사 트레이너'로도 활약하고 있다.

저서

라이언 쌤, 이렇게 가르쳐서 영어 수업 대박내다 (성우) / 하룻밤에 보는 영문법 (뉴런) / 나도 미드로 영어공부하고 싶다 (뉴런)
고등학교 영어 교과서 1, 2 (두산동아) / 영문법 훈련노트 1, 2 (길벗이지톡)

라이언 쌤, 이렇게 가르쳐서
영어수업 대박내다 Ⅱ - 활동편

1판 1쇄 인쇄 2012년 8월 10일 | **1판 6쇄 발행** 2019년 12월 5일 | **지은이** 박용호 | **펴낸이** 주성우 | **펴낸곳** 도서출판 성우
출판등록 1999년 9월 28일 제 22-1629호 | **마케팅 부장** 주영웅 | **마케팅** 손귀자 백승우 | **인쇄** 사이삼피앤피
주소 경기도 안양시 동안구 시민대로 401 대륭테크노타운 15차 1306호 | **전화번호** 031-389-8800~3 | **팩스** 031-389-8888
전자우편 sungwoobook@sungwoobook.com | **홈페이지** www.sungwoobook.com
ISBN 978-89-5885-312-1 13740

ⓒ 도서출판 성우

도서출판 성우의 허락없이 이 책에 실린 글과 사진, 그림의 일부 또는 전체를 인용하거나 발췌하는 것을 금합니다.

라이언 쌤,
이렇게 가르쳐서

영어수업
대박내다

활동편

Ⅱ

글 박용호 | 그림 주예나 외

도서출판 성우

오페라 : 드디어 "라이언 쌤, 이렇게 가르쳐서 영어 수업 대박내다"의 두 번째 책이 나왔네요. 얼마만이죠?

라이언 쌤 : 첫 책이 2007년에 나왔으니까 거의 5년만이죠.

오페라 : 첫 책에 대한 반응이 항상 궁금했어요. 그 책이 여태까지 나온 책들하고는 좀 달랐잖아요.

라이언 쌤 : 현장에 있는 영어 교사를 위한 책으로는 거의 처음이지 않았나 생각이 드는데요. 현장 경험을 바탕으로 쓴 책이라서 그런지 영어 선생님들께서 많은 관심을 가져 주셨어요. 그리고 좋은 영어 선생님을 꿈꾸는 미래의 영어 교사들에게 많은 도움을 받고 있다는 말도 자주 들었습니다. 그러니까 이렇게 두 번째 책이 나오게 되었겠죠?

오페라 : 이번 책도 선생님의 경험을 바탕으로 하는 책인가요? 어떤 책인지 소개 좀 해 주세요.

라이언 쌤 : 물론이죠. "라이언 쌤" 1편은 대한민국에서 영어를 잘 가르치기 위한 전반적인 지식에 관한 것이었구요. 이번 2편은 좀 더 구체적으로 선생님들께서 수업 시간에 사용할 수 있는 다양한 활동을 소개하고 있습니다. ice breaker, speaking, writing, grammar, vocabulary의 5개 영역에서 각각 10개의 활동을 소개하고 있는데요. 총 50가지의 다양하고 흥미로운 영어 활동을 만나보실 수 있는거죠.

오페라 : 50가지의 영어 활동이라... 어디서 그런 아이디어를 얻으세요?

라이언 쌤 : 영어는 학문이 아니라 "말"하는 것이잖아요. 그러니까 당연히 저의 일상 생활에서 많은 아이디어를 얻습니다. 가령 "Order Your Sandwich" 활동은 제가 미국 샌드위치 가게에서 주문하는 것이 너무 힘들어서 고생했던 경험을 바탕으로 만든 것이구요, "Konglish vs English" 활동도 당당하게 Konglish를 영어처럼 사용하는 저희 학생들을 보고 만든 것입니다. 그리고 어렸을 때 했던 battleship등의 게임들이나 제가 과거 영어를 배우면서 했던 활동들도 제 수업 아이디어의 밑거름이 된답니다. 우리에게 친숙한 것들을 수업시간에 사용하게 되면 좀 더 쉽게 영어 활동에 참여할 수 있거든요. 아, 그리고 이 책을 쓰기 위해서 제가 참고한 것들은 활동 소개 글의 맨 밑에 출처를 밝혀 두었습니다.

오페라 : 책의 구성이 참 독특합니다. 이런 구성은 다른 책에서는 잘 보지 못했거든요.

라이언 쌤 : 외국에서는 이런 책을 photocopiable book이라고 합니다. 책에 있는 자료들을 교육적인 목적에서 선생님들께서 마음껏 복사해서 학생들에게 나눠 줄 수 있도록 한 것이죠. 담임업무, 공문처리 등으로 너무 바쁜 영어 선생님들께서 활동에 필요한 worksheet을 따로 만들지 말고 이 책에 있는 worksheet을 그냥 복사만해서 쓰시도록 한 것입니다. 책의 왼쪽 부분에 활동을 어떻게 하는지 소개해 두었구요, 책의 오른쪽 부분에 worksheet을 실어 두었습니다. 그리고 영어로 수업을 진행하는 것에 자신이 없으신 영어 선생님들을 위해서 활동을 영어로 진행하는 법을 따로 적어 두었습니다.

오페라 : 사실 요즘 영어로 진행하는 영어 수업, 실용영어 강화정책 등으로 영어 선생님들께서 힘드실 것 같은데요. 요즘 어떠세요?

라이언 쌤 : 선생님들 뿐만 아니라 인간이라면 자신의 comfort zone을 깨고 변화를 시도한다는 것이 100% 반가운 것만은 아니죠. 하지만 지금까지의 영어 교육이 문법이나 수동적인 해석만을 강조한 나머지 학생들을 벙어리로 만들어 버린 것은 사실이잖아요. 지금이라도 학교 현장에서 학생들의 입을 열게 하는 수업방법이 많이 도입되어야 한다고 생각합니다. 실제로 그런 수업을 현장에서 진행하고 있는 교사들도 많이 있거든요. 이 책은 그런 아이디어를 영어 선생님들과 공유하고자 하는 의미로 만든 것이지요.

오페라 : 앞으로 라이언 쌤의 꿈은 뭔가요? 최고의 교사가 되는 것?

라이언 쌤 : 저는 절대로 최고의 교사는 될 수는 없다고 생각을 합니다. 대신 "최고로 고민을 많이 하는" 교사가 되고 싶습니다. 아이들이 행복해 하는 수업을 만들기 위해서 치열하게 고민하는 선생님이 되고 싶은 거죠. 아이들이 제 이름은 기억을 못하더라도 제 수업을 통해서 배운 것들을 나중에 써 먹을 수 있으면 그걸로 행복한 거죠.

오페라 : 그럼 마지막으로 라이언 쌤의 제자들에게 영상 편지 한번 띄우시죠.

라이언 쌤 : 좋은 교사가 좋은 학생을 만드는 것처럼 좋은 학생이 좋은 교사를 만든다고 하잖아. 나같이 빈틈이 많은 교사에게 좋은 교사가 되는 꿈을 가지도록 해 주는 너희들은 정말 훌륭한 학생들이란다. 항상 고맙고 많이 못해 줘서 미안하고… 그리고… 사랑한다!

UNIT 1

Ice Breaker
Activities

UNIT 1 Ice Breaker Activities

1-1	Classroom English (p.8 ~ p.9)
Type	Group work
Aim	To practice classroom English
Level	Beginner ~ pre-intermediate
Time	10 ~ 20 minutes

1-2	We Found Our Group (p.10 ~ p.13)
Type	Group work
Aim	To make groups of students
Level	All level
Time	5 ~ 7 minutes

1-3	Are You a Happy Student? (p.14 ~ p.15)
Type	Solo work
Aim	Self-check of their school life
Level	Beginner ~ intermediate
Time	10 minutes

1-4	What Did You Do Last Weekend? (p.16 ~ p.17)
Type	Pair work
Aim	To talk about their weekends
Level	Pre-intermediate
Time	5 ~ 7 minutes

1-5	Answer Our Questions (p.18 ~ p.19)
Type	Group work
Aim	To get to know each other
Level	Pre-intermediate ~ intermediate
Time	10 minutes

1-6	Survey Show (p.20 ~ p.21)
Type	Group work
Aim	To guess the survey results
Level	Pre-intermediate ~ intermediate
Time	10 minutes

1-7	Crazy Juliet (p.22 ~ p.23)
Type	Pair work
Aim	To make sentences with a partner
Level	All level
Time	7 ~ 10 minutes

1-8	Me & You (p.24 ~ p.25)
Type	Pair work
Aim	To get to know each other
Level	Pre-intermediate ~ intermediate
Time	15 minutes

1-9	Pass & Score (p.26 ~ p.27)
Type	Group work
Aim	To talk about myself
Level	Beginner ~ pre-intermediate
Time	10 minutes

1-10	Certificate & Award (p.28 ~ p.29)
Type	Group work
Aim	To present certificates and awards to students
Level	All level
Time	20 minutes

1-1

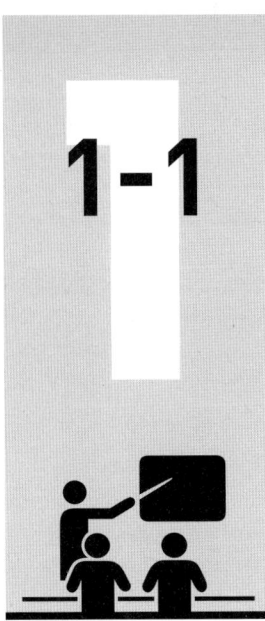

🔺 Ice Breaker Activities

Classroom English

Type
Group work / Ice breaker

Aim
To practice classroom English

Level
Beginner ~ pre-intermediate

Time
10 ~ 20 minutes

Language
Classroom English expressions

How to do the activity

1. 4명의 학생들이 한 모둠이 되도록 합니다.
2. 9쪽에 있는 classroom English 표현과 뜻 카드를 잘라 각 모둠에 나누어 줍니다. 각 모둠의 학생들은 협동을 통해서 영어 표현과 뜻을 연결하는 활동을 합니다.
3. 학생들의 활동이 끝나면 교사와 함께 정답을 맞추도록 합니다. 하반의 경우 영어 표현을 읽는 것도 연습하도록 합니다.
4. 각 모둠에서 classroom English 표현 카드는 따로 모아 놓고 한국어로 뜻이 적힌 카드만 책상 위에 올려 두도록 합니다.
5. 교사가 English 카드 중 하나를 읽으면 각 모둠의 학생들은 그의 뜻에 해당하는 한글 표현 카드를 재빨리 집어야 합니다. 가장 많은 한글 표현 카드를 집은 학생이 그 모둠의 승자가 됩니다. 승자는 오늘 배운 교실 영어 표현과 뜻을 쓰는 숙제를 면제 받게 됩니다.

Teacher's Talk

1. I'm going to give you two types of cards; one of them is a classroom English card and the other one is a meaning card. Within your group, you need to match the English cards with the correct meaning cards. I'll give you one minute to match your cards.
2. Good job! Let's check your answers now, shall we?
3. Now, put away the classroom English cards and leave the meaning cards on the desk.
4. I'm going to read one of the classroom English expressions. Listen carefully and then pick up the right meaning card. The person who collects the most cards will be the winner within your group. As a reward, the winners don't need to do homework today.

Ryan's Tip

1. 학생들이 영어로 진행하는 수업을 쉽게 이해하기 위해서는 교사가 자주 사용하는 영어 표현을 익히도록 하는 과정이 필요합니다. 물론 이 과정이 없어도 학생들이 눈치껏 영어 표현들을 이해할 수도 있겠지만 그러기에는 시간이 다소 걸리기도 하고, 포기하는 아이들도 생기게 되지요. 그래서 이런 활동을 준비했습니다. 이 활동은 가급적이면 새 학기에 시작하시는 것이 좋습니다.
2. 영어 표현과 뜻을 연결한 후에는 학생들이 각자 이 표현들을 익힐 수 있는 시간을 주는 것도 좋습니다. 특히 하반의 경우 이 과정이 필요합니다.

1-1 Classroom English

What you need to do is ~	여러분이 할 일은 ~ 입니다.
The first thing that we're going to do is ~	우리가 할 첫 번째 것은 ~ 입니다.
Wrap it up!	자, 마무리 하세요.
May I have your attention?	주목해 주세요.
Put away your book.	책을 치우세요.
Don't chit-chat with your friends.	친구들과 잡담하지 마세요.
Let's move on to the next activity.	이제 다음 활동을 해 봅시다.
Take a look at ~.	~ 를 보세요.
Let's review what we talked about in our last class.	지난 시간에 한 것이 무엇인지 복습해 봅시다.
Let me give you an example.	예를 들어 설명해 보겠습니다.
Today's topic is about ~	오늘의 주제는 ~에 관한 것입니다.
Check your answers with a partner.	정답을 짝과 맞추어 봅시다.
Raise your hand if you have a question.	질문이 있으면 손을 드세요.
Work in groups.	모둠으로 활동하세요.
Stand in front of the class.	앞에 나가서 서 있으세요.
Speak up, please!	크게 이야기 해 줄래요!
Sit up straight!	똑바로 앉으세요.

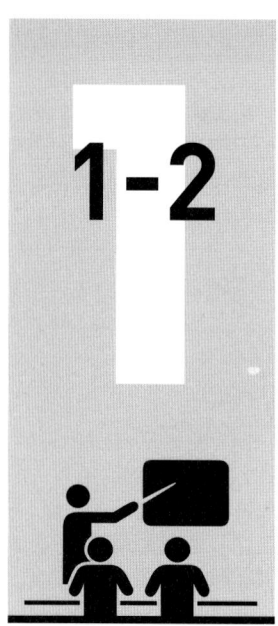

Ice Breaker Activities

1-2 We Found Our Group!

Type of activity
Group work / Ice breaker

Aim of activity
To make groups of students

Level
All level

Time
5 ~ 7 minutes

Target language
Vocabulary of subjects, animals, plants, furniture, weather and food

How to do the activity

1. 이 활동은 학생들을 grouping 할 때 사용할 수 있는 활동입니다.
2. 만들고 싶은 조의 수와 조의 인원에 따라 11~13쪽의 영어 단어 카드를 잘라 준비해 둡니다. 예를 들어 6명으로 구성된 5개의 조를 만든다고 가정해 봅시다. 그러면 subject, animal, plant, furniture, weather의 5개의 그룹 단어를 각각 6개씩 잘라 총 30개의 단어 카드를 만들면 됩니다. 이번에는 5명으로 구성된 6개의 조를 만든다고 가정해 보면 subject, animal, plant, furniture, weather, food의 6개의 그룹단어를 각각 5개씩 잘라 총 30개의 카드를 만들도록 합니다. 이 때 각 그룹에 있는 1개의 카드는 학생들에게 나누어 주어서는 안되겠지요.
3. 학생 수대로 잘라서 준비한 영어 단어 카드를 학생들에게 한 장씩 나누어 줍니다. 자신의 카드가 무엇인지 확인 한 후 카드를 자신의 주머니 속에 집어 넣도록 합니다.
4. 학생들은 모두 일어 서서 자신이 가지고 있는 단어 카드와 비슷한 종류의 카드를 가진 학생을 찾아야 합니다. 가령 science 카드를 가지고 있는 학생은 English, math 등 과목과 관련된 카드를 가지고 있는 학생들을 찾아야 하고, lion 카드를 가지고 있는 학생은 tiger, dog 등 동물과 관련된 카드를 가지고 있는 학생들을 찾아야 합니다. 자신의 부류를 모두 찾은 학생들은 크게 "We found our group!" 이라고 외칩니다. 가장 먼저 자신의 부류를 찾은 팀이 승리하게 됩니다.
5. 주머니 속에 있던 카드를 꺼내어 자신의 부류가 맞는지 확인하도록 합니다.

Teacher's Talk

1. Today, we're going to make five different groups of six students. To make these groups, we're going to play a game.
2. I'm going to give each of you a card that has an English word and a picture. Look at your card and then put it in your pocket.
3. (After giving cards to the students) Now, you need to stand up and ask your friends what kind of card he/she has. When you find a student with a card in a similar category, that student is your group member. For example, let's say Jenny has an "English" card, Kim has a "math" card, and Susan has a "lion" card. Jenny and Kim belong to the same group, but Susan doesn't because she belongs to the "animal" group.
4. When you find all six group members, say, "We found our group!" The first three groups who say, "We found our group!" are the winners of the game. Once again, you have to find six students who have the similar category card. Ready? Everybody, stand up! Begin!

1-2 We Found Our Group

[Group : Subject]

English	math	science
music	art	physical education

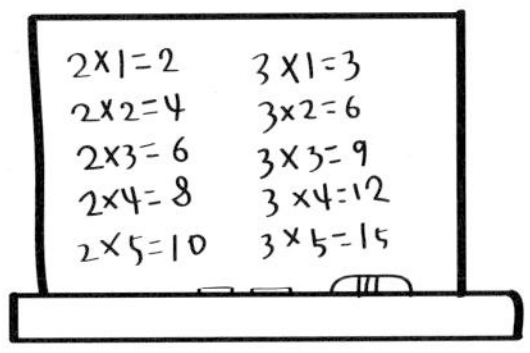

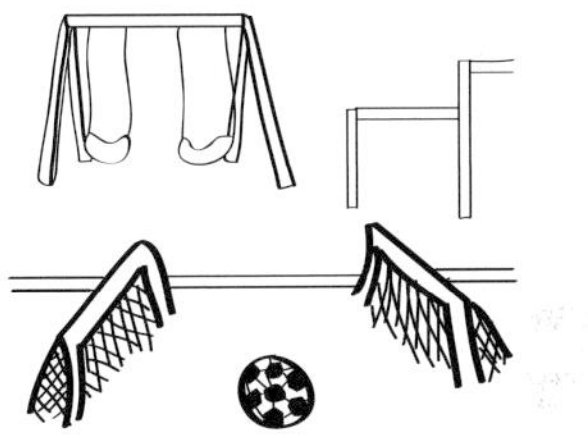

[Group : Animal]

penguin	lion	tiger
dog	rabbit	monkey

Ice Breaker Activities

[Group : Plant]

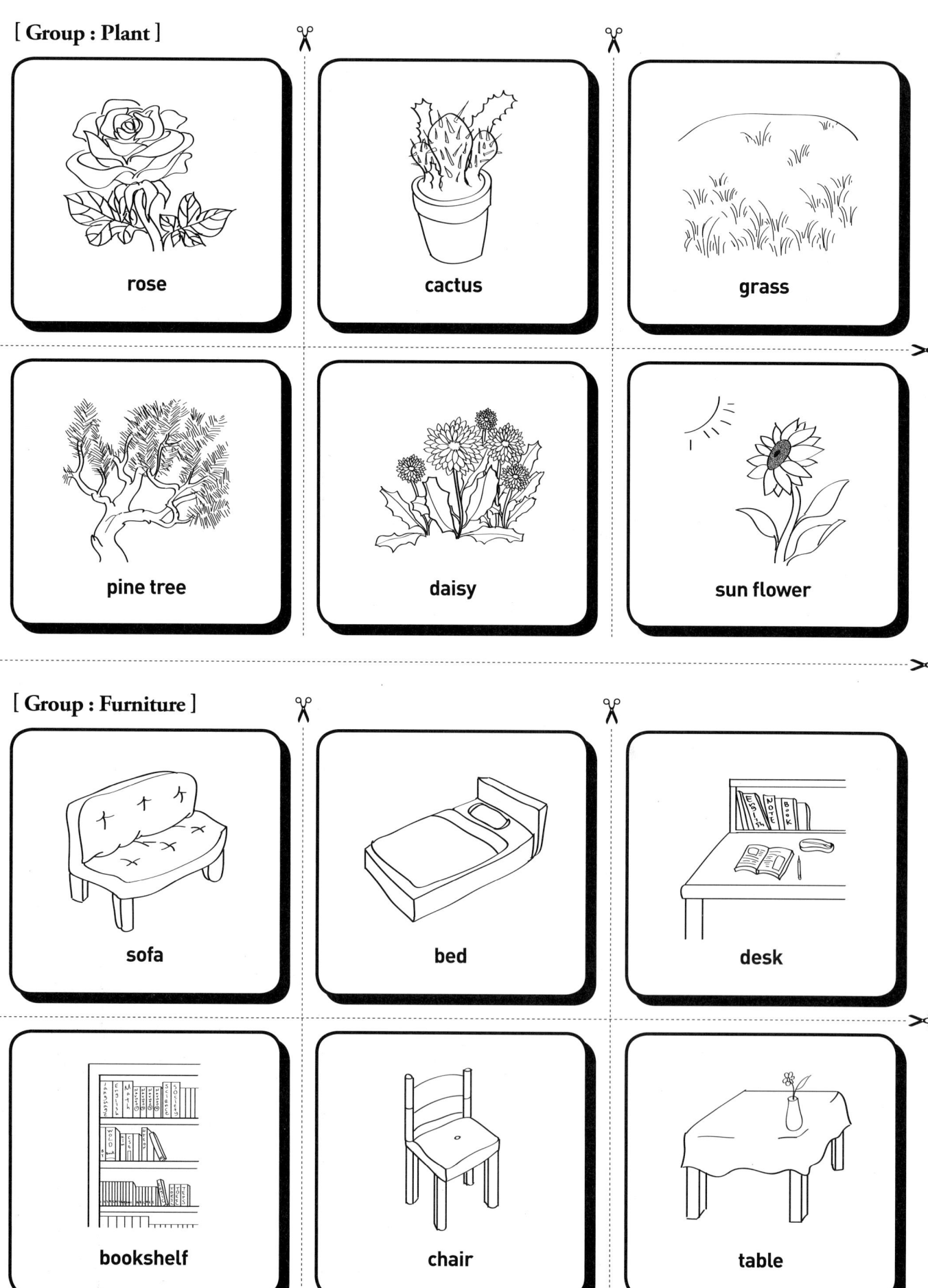

1-3 Are You a Happy Student?

🔺 Ice Breaker Activities

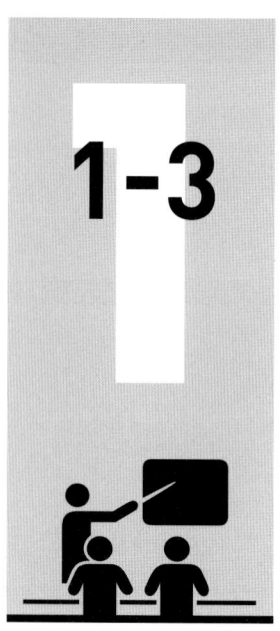

Type
Solo work / Ice breaker

Aim
Self-check of their school life

Level
Beginner ~ intermediate

Time
10 minutes

Language
Feeling vocabulary / daily routines in school

How to do the activity

1. 학생들에게 15쪽의 worksheet 을 나누어 줍니다.
2. 학교 생활에 대한 15개의 항목을 읽고 자신에 해당하는 감정에 체크(V) 하도록 합니다. 각 항목의 체크가 끝나면 총점을 더하도록 합니다.
3. 교사가 총점에 따른 Happy School Life 지표 (아래 표)를 읽어 줍니다.
4. worksheet 아래에 각 지수에 맞게 학교 생활을 재미있게 할 수 있는 방법들을 간단하게 적어 보고 학생들과 이야기해 보도록 합니다.

Teacher's Talk

1. On the worksheet, you'll see 15 sentences about school life. Read them and then check (V) how you feel about them. When you're finished, add up the scores and write down the total score at the bottom of the chart.
2. Raise your hand if your total score is from 45 to 35. According to the Happy School Life Chart, you're .... (Read the chart below)
3. Now, let's think about what we can do to make our school life better. Think about action plans based on your score. Write them on the worksheet that I gave you. For example, if your score is high, think of something that you can do to help other students in school. Maybe you can be a school president or a club captain. If your score is too low, think about how to get some help from others.

Your score	Your School Life
45 ~ 35	You're a perfect role model of a student. You're loved by everyone in school including teachers and fellow students. Why don't you run for student president? You can help other students who struggle with their school life.
34 ~ 25	You're doing okay in school. You don't hate school, but you don't have a particular reason to go to school, either. There are many things you can do in school besides studying. How about joining a club?
24 ~ 15	You seem to be negative about your school. Change your attitude! Try to find a friend whom you can share your feelings with. Go and talk to your classmates. They will not bite you. Also, your teachers are there to help you.

1-3 Are You a Happy Student?

Are You a Happy Student?

Read the following sentences about school life and then check (V) how you feel.

Your school life	Happy (3 points) ☺	Okay (2 points) 😐	Unhappy (1 points) ☹
meet new classmates during the new school year			
have English class			
read books in the library			
give a speech in public			
work in a team (or in a pair)			
play sports or games in PE class			
have music class			
go on a school trip			
have lunch in school			
come to school every morning			
talk to your homeroom teacher			
ask your parents to come to school			
have extra-curricular classes (after school)			
study for a math test			
go to a school festival (dance party)			
total score			

Total score : _____

What can you do to make your school life better? Write your action plans.

Your Score	Your action plan
	* I'll _____ * I'll _____ _____ _____

라이언 쌤, 이렇게 가르쳐서 영어수업 대박내다 Ⅱ - **활동편**

1-4 What Did You Do Last Weekend?

Ice Breaker Activities

Type
Pair work / Ice breaker

Aim
To talk about their weekends

Level
Pre-intermediate

Time
5~7 minutes

Language
Vocabulary of daily routines

How to do the activity

1. 학생들에게 지난 주말에 무슨 일을 했는지 잠시 생각하도록 합니다.

2. 17쪽의 worksheet을 잘라서 학생들에게 나누어 줍니다. 학생들은 자신이 받은 worksheet을 다른 학생들에게 보여 주어서는 안됩니다.

3. 학생들 모두가 일어서서 3명의 학생에게 지난 주말에 무슨 일을 했는지 물어보고 그 대답을 worksheet에 적도록 합니다.
이 때 주의할 것은 상대 학생의 대답이 No! No!에 나와 있는 표현과 유사하거나 일치할 경우에는 "No! No!"라고 크게 말합니다. 이렇게 될 경우 그 학생은 주말에 했던 또 다른 일을 말해야 합니다. 예를 들어 상대 학생이 "I watched a movie."라고 대답을 했는데 그 대답이 No! No!에 나와 있는 것이면 그 학생은 다른 활동을 말해 주어야 한다는 것입니다.

4. 활동이 끝난 뒤 각자가 적은 worksheet을 이용하여 다른 학생들이 주말에 무슨 일을 했는지 말해보는 시간을 가지도록 합니다.

Teacher's Talk

1. Close your eyes and think about what you did last weekend. You need to have in mind at least 3 activities that you did last weekend.

2. Now, I'm going to give you this worksheet. What you need to do is to stand up and then find 3 different people. Ask them what they did last weekend and then write their answers on the worksheet. You need to ask three different people what they did last weekend and write their answers on the worksheet. It seems to be a simple activity, however, it's not that easy. If your friend's answer is similar to the No! No! on your worksheet, your friend should tell you something different. Suppose that your friend says, "I watched a movie." If "watching a movie" is a No! No! on your worksheet, you should say "No! No!" and your friend should say something else.

Ryan's Tip

1. 하반의 경우 "What did you do last weekend?"라는 질문에 대부분의 학생들이 "I watched TV." 혹은 "I played computer games." 등의 틀에 박힌 대답을 하는 경우가 많으므로 이 활동을 생각하게 되었습니다.

2. 학생들이 일어서서 하는 짝 활동의 경우에는 교사의 세심한 monitoring이 더욱 필요합니다. 특히 소극적인 학생들이 자발적으로 참여하지 않을 경우에는 약간의 강제성을 발휘하여 교사가 직접 pair를 정해주는 것도 필요합니다.

1-4 What Did You Do Last Weekend?

What did you do last weekend?	
No! No! : watch TV / study / play with friends / go to hakwon	
Friend's name	What they did

What did you do last weekend?	
No! No! : sleep / watch TV / computer / go to hakwon	
Friend's name	What they did

What did you do last weekend?	
No! No! : play with friends / go to church / go to Jimjilbang / sleep	
Friend's name	What they did

What did you do last weekend?	
No! No! : dinner with family / do homework / go to church / game	
Friend's name	What they did

What did you do last weekend?	
No! No! : do homework / play sports / watch TV / computer	
Friend's name	What they did

1-5 Answer Our Questions

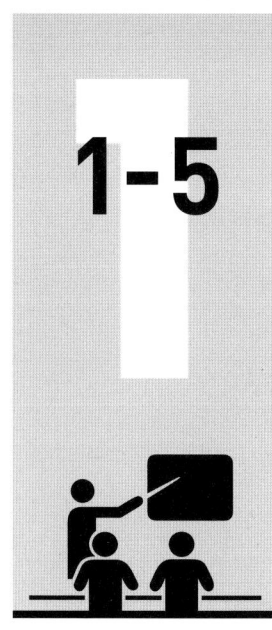

Ice Breaker Activities

Type
Group work / Ice breaker

Aim
To get to know each other

Level
Pre-intermediate ~ intermediate

Time
10 minutes

Language
Questions

How to do the activity

1. 교실 앞에 의자를 하나 둡니다.
2. 장난감 악어의 이빨을 학생들이 하나씩 누르도록 합니다. 악어의 입이 갑자기 닫히면 그 학생이 의자에 앉아야 합니다.
3. 다른 학생들에게 19쪽의 질문지를 잘라서 하나씩 나누어 줍니다. 2분 동안 학생들은 자신의 질문지에 있는 의문문 형식을 이용하여 의자에 앉아있는 학생에게 물어볼 질문 2가지를 만듭니다.
4. 4명의 학생이 한 조가 되어 자신이 만든 질문을 공유하고 그 조에서 가장 재미있는 질문을 하나 선정합니다.
5. 각 조에서 선정한 질문을 의자에 앉아 있는 학생에게 질문합니다. 이 때 그 학생은 정직하게 질문에 답해야 하는데 불편을 느끼거나, 지극히 개인적인 질문에 대해서는 "Sorry"을 사용할 수 있습니다. 단 Sorry를 사용하는 횟수는 1회로 제한되어 있으니 신중하게 써야 합니다.

Teacher's Talk

1. (Putting a chair in front of the class) One of you will sit in this chair and answer questions from the other students. I'm going to pass this crocodile around, and each of you must push one tooth down. If the crocodile gets angry and catches your finger, you should take the seat.
2. (After choosing a student for the seat) Now, I'm going to give you a worksheet. You need to make two questions for *Kiho* (the student on the seat), using the provided question form.
3. Make groups of four students. Compare your questions and then choose the best question for *Kiho*. You may choose only one question in your group.
4. It's time to ask your questions to *Kiho*. *Kiho*, you have one *Sorry*. If you think the question is too offensive, you can say "*Sorry*," and you don't need to answer it. However, you should be very careful to use your *Sorry* wisely because you have only one chance to use it. Okay, Group 1, what's your question for Kiho?

Ryan's Tip

1. 이 활동은 ice breaker 뿐만 아니라 question form을 가르치는 문법 시간에도 사용할 수 있습니다. 가령 "How many times~?"를 target language로 가르쳤다면 "How many times~"만 이용하여 질문을 만들도록 하는 것입니다. 이렇게 되면 controlled grammar activity가 되는 거겠죠?
2. 전학생 등의 새로운 학생이 수업에 참여하는 경우에도 쉽게 할 수 있는 활동입니다.

1-5 Answer Our Questions

Make two questions using the question form below.
When ~?

e.g.) When did you graduate from kindergarten?

1. When _____?
1. When _____?

Make two questions using the question form below.
How many ~?

e.g.) How many brothers and sisters do you have?

1. How many _____?
1. How many _____?

Make two questions using the question form below.
How often ~?

e.g.) How often do you watch movies?

1. How often _____?
1. How often _____?

Make two questions using the question form below.
What do you think about ~?

e.g.) What do you think about our class leader?

1. What do you think about _____?
1. What do you think about _____?

Make two questions using the question form below.
What would you do if ~?

e.g.) What would you do if you were rich?

1. What would you do if _____?
1. What would you do if _____?

라이언 쌤, 이렇게 가르쳐서 영어수업 대박내다 Ⅱ - 활동편

1-6 Survey Show

Ice Breaker Activities

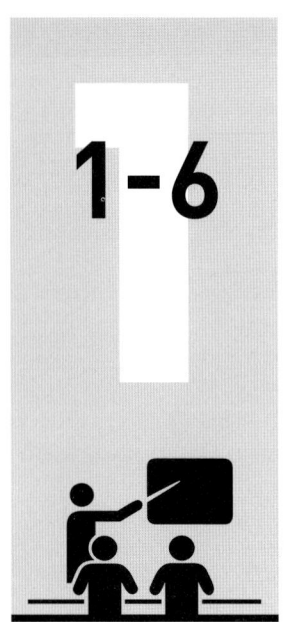

Type
Group work / Ice breaker

Aim
To guess the survey results

Level
Pre-intermediate ~ intermediate

Time
10 minutes

Language
I think ~ / In my opinion ~ (see the table below)

How to do the activity

1. 이 활동은 theme-based 수업에서 사용하면 좋습니다. 가령 cooking과 관련된 수업이면 "What's your favorite food?"에 대한 설문 결과를, feeling과 관련된 수업이면 "When are you happy?" 라는 설문 결과를 사용하도록 합니다.

2. 4명이 한 모둠이 되도록 합니다. 각 모둠의 학생들은 설문 조사 질문에 대한 Top 5 대답을 추측을 통해서 맞추어야 합니다. 각 모둠에 2~3분 정도의 시간을 주고 자신들의 추측을 적을 수 있도록 합니다. 순위에 상관 없이 많은 아이디어를 적도록 합니다.

3. 3분 뒤 전체 학생들이 Top 5 대답을 맞추도록 합니다. 가장 많은 대답을 맞춘 모둠이 승리 팀이 됩니다.

Teacher's Talk

1. Today, we're going to talk about cooking. The first activity that we're going to do is called "Survey Show." As a survey, I asked 100 high school students, "What's your favorite food?" and I have the list of their top five answers. What you need to do is guess what the top five answers are. You need to work with your team members.

2. I'm going to give you a worksheet. On the worksheet, write as many guesses as possible. It's better to write more than five guesses. I'm going to give you three minutes.

3. (Three minutes later) Put your pens down, everyone. Now, tell me your guesses. What do you think their favorite food is? Anyone?

Ryan's Tip

1. 학생들이 정답을 이야기 할 때 target language를 이용하도록 유도하기 바랍니다. 각 survey에 대한 target language는 다음과 같습니다.

Survey	Target language
Favorite food	I think they like to eat _____ most.
Christmas present	I think they want _____ for Christmas.
Happy	I think they are happy when _____ .
Free time	I think they like to _____ in their free time.
Future job	I think they want to be _____ .
First date	I think they want to _____ on their first date.

Do NOT give this copy to students. This is the survey result.
Student should guess the results with their group members.

Survey Results

- Respondents : 100 high school students (boys + girls)
- Date of Survey : April 11, 2011

What's your favorite food?

1. meat
2. pizza
3. mom's recipe
4. spaghetti
5. Tokboki

What do you want for Christmas?

1. money
2. boy / girlfriend
3. cell phone
4. MP3
5. clothes

When are you happy?

1. getting good grades
2. no school day
3. sleeping
4. dating
5. meeting friends

What do you do in your free time?

1. computer
2. hanging out with friends
3. sleeping
4. watching movies
5. watching TV

What's your favorite subject?

1. music
2. physical education
3. English
4. Computer
5. Korean

What do you want to do on your first date?

1. going for a walk
2. watching a movie
3. going to a concert (musical)
4. eating delicious food
5. kissing

1-7 Crazy Juliet

Ice Breaker Activities

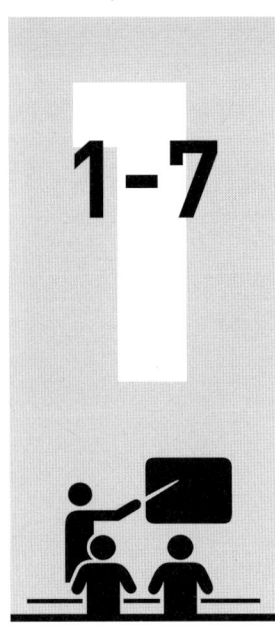

Type
Pair work / Ice breaker

Aim
To make sentences with a partner

Level
All level

Time
7 ~ 10 minutes

Language
noun / verb / adjective / adverb

How to do the activity

1. 두 명이 한 조가 되도록 한 뒤 Romeo와 Juliet을 정하도록 합니다. Romeo는 23쪽의 worksheet을 받습니다. 절대 Juliet에게 worksheet을 보여 주어서는 안 됩니다.

2. Romeo는 Juliet에게 빈칸에 필요한 단어를 임의로 불러달라고 합니다. 이때 사용하는 말은 "Juliet, I want your _____." 입니다. 예를 들어, 형용사가 필요해서 형용사를 달라고 할 때는 "Juliet, I want your adjective."라고 말합니다. 그러면 Juliet은 많은 생각을 하지 말고 바로 생각나는 형용사를 하나 불러 줍니다.

3. Romeo는 Juliet이 불러주는 단어들을 빈칸에 적습니다. 이런 방식으로 단어들을 적다 보면 하나의 글이 완성됩니다.

4. 글이 완성되면 Juliet에게 보여 준 뒤 Juliet이 가장 재미있는 문장을 하나 선택하도록 합니다. 자신들이 선택한 재미있는 문장을 다른 학생들에게 읽어 줍니다.

Teacher's Talk

1. I'm going to put you in pairs. You need to decide who is Romeo and who is Juliet in your pair.

2. Romeo will get this worksheet. Don't show it to your Juliet.

3. Romeo will say this; Juliet, I want your XXXX. Juliet should give what Romeo asks. For example, let's say I'm Romeo and she *(one of the students)* is my Juliet. I say, "I want your noun." Then she needs to give me any noun that she can think of immediately. If my Juliet says "apple" then I will write apple in the blank.

4. You need to work together until Romeo fills up all the blanks on the worksheet. Remember, Romeo, You MUST NOT show your worksheet to Juliet.

5. (5~7 minutes later) Okay, Romeo, show your worksheet to Juliet. Juliet, choose the funniest sentence that you've just made with Romeo.

Ryan's Tip

1. 활동을 하기 전에 noun, verb, adjective, adverb를 영어로 어떻게 읽는지, 그 뜻이 무엇인지 가르쳐 주세요. 하반의 경우는 단어를 생각해서 말하는 것이 힘들 수 있으므로 여러 단어를 예시로 준 뒤 그 중에서 하나를 선택할 수 있도록 해 주세요.

*출처 : 이 활동은 미국의 유명한 게임인 Mad Libs 에서 아이디어를 얻었습니다

Crazy Juliet

⟨Sample dialog⟩
Romeo : Juliet, I want your *noun*.
Juliet : *apple*

I want to tell you about myself.

1. I like to eat _____. Also, I can cook _____ very well.
　　　　　　　　　(noun)　　　　　　　　　　　　　　　　　　　(noun)

2. My room is very _____. I love my room.
　　　　　　　　　(adjective)

3. I like to _____ my friends. My friends love me so much.
　　　　　(verb)

4. My friends call me _____. My partner's nickname is _____.
　　　　　　　　　　(noun)　　　　　　　　　　　　　　　　　　　　(noun)

5. On weekends, I like to _____, but I don't like to _____.
　　　　　　　　　　　(verb)　　　　　　　　　　　　　　　　　(verb)

6. I think I look like a/an _____. Sometimes, I smell like a/an _____.
　　　　　　　　　　　(noun)　　　　　　　　　　　　　　　　　　　(noun)

7. I want to have a/an _____ in my room. It can be a nice pet.
　　　　　　　　　　　(animal)

8. I want to marry a person like _____. I like him/her because he/she can _____ well.
　　　　　　　　　　　　　(person's name)　　　　　　　　　　　　　　　　　(verb)

9. Before going to bed, I always _____.
　　　　　　　　　　　　　　　　(verb)

10. In the future, I want to be a/an _____ husband/wife. I want to have _____ children.
　　　　　　　　　　　　　　　(adjective)　　　　　　　　　　　　　(number)

Which sentence is the funniest? Choose one.

Sentence # _____

1-8 Me & You

Ice Breaker Activities

Type
Pair work / Ice breaker

Aim
To get to know each other

Level
Pre-intermediate ~ intermediate

Time
15 minutes

Language
Questions

How to do the activity

1. 짝으로 진행하는 활동입니다. 학생들에게 25쪽의 worksheet을 잘라서 나누어 줍니다.
2. 각 학생들은 여러 가지 질문을 통해서 자신과 짝과의 공통점과 차이점을 찾아야 합니다. 발견한 공통점, 차이점을 worksheet에 간단하게 적도록 합니다. 공통점은 두 원이 만나는 칸 안에, 차이점은 두 원이 만나지 않는 각각의 칸 안에 쓰도록 합니다. 단, 누구나 공감하는 공통점, 예를 들어 성별, 나이, 학교 등은 쓰지 않도록 합니다.
3. 짝과의 활동이 끝나면 교사는 학생들이 발견한 공통점과 차이점을 물어봅니다.
4. 3명을 한 모둠으로 정하고 그들의 공통점과 차이점을 찾아보는 활동을 과제로 줄 수도 있습니다.

Teacher's Talk

1. I'm going to give you this worksheet. You need to find what you and your partner have in common by asking a lot of questions to your partner. For example, ask him/her how many sisters he/she has. If he/she has the same number of sisters, write the number in the center of the diagrams. If it's different, write different numbers in each diagram.
2. The very common similarities such as age, gender, or current school name should be excluded from this activity.

Ryan's Tip

1. 하반 학생들의 경우 개인 신상을 물어볼 수 있는 질문 (How many ~? Where were you born? 등)을 미리 학습한 후 활동을 진행하는 것이 좋습니다. 또한 "What's your favorite ~?"과 같이 질문의 주제를 한정해 주는 것도 좋습니다.
2. 학생들의 활동을 monitoring 할 때 학생들의 영어에서 error를 발견했다고 해서 그 자리에서 바로 고쳐주지 마세요. 따로 적어두었다가 활동이 끝난 뒤 error correction을 하는 것이 좋습니다. 가급적 학생들 활동의 흐름을 끊지 않기 위해서랍니다. error correction을 할 때도 학생의 이름을 밝히지 않고 그냥 error를 칠판에 적은 후 어떤 곳이 잘못되었고 어떻게 고쳐야 하는지 학생들 스스로가 파악할 수 있도록 해 주세요. 이름을 밝히지 않아도 실수를 한 아이는 자신의 실수를 알아 볼 수 있습니다.

Me & You

Find similar and different things about you and your partner by asking questions.

e.g.) hobby / hometown / favorite subject / favorite star / places I like to go to / friends...

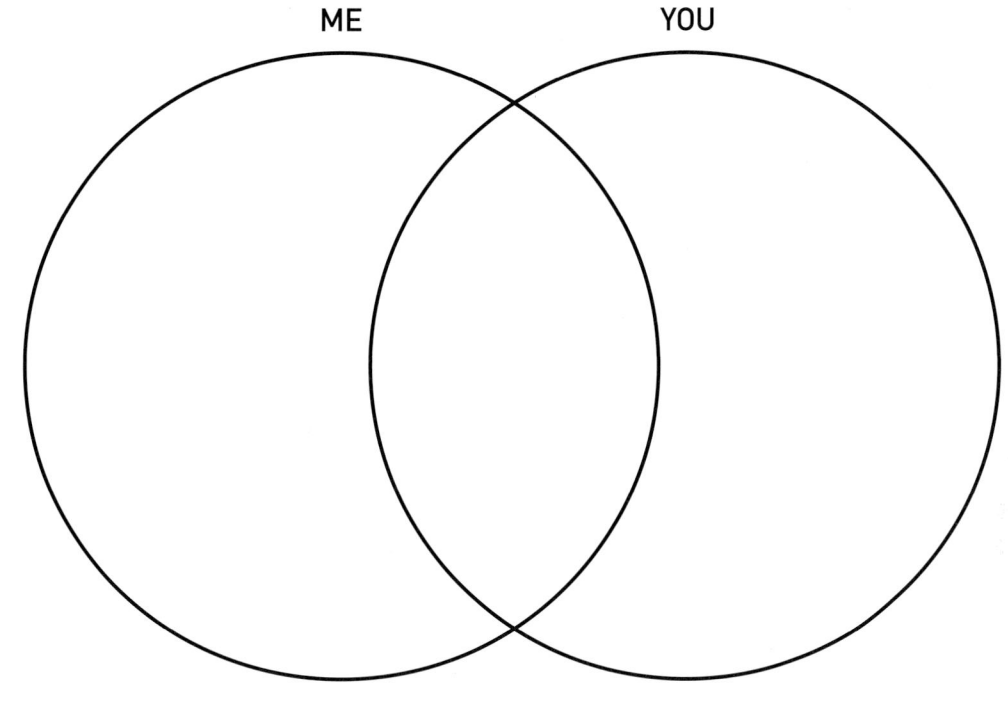

Me & You

Find similar and different things about you and your partner by asking questions.

e.g.) hobby / hometown / favorite subject / favorite star / places I like to go to / friends...

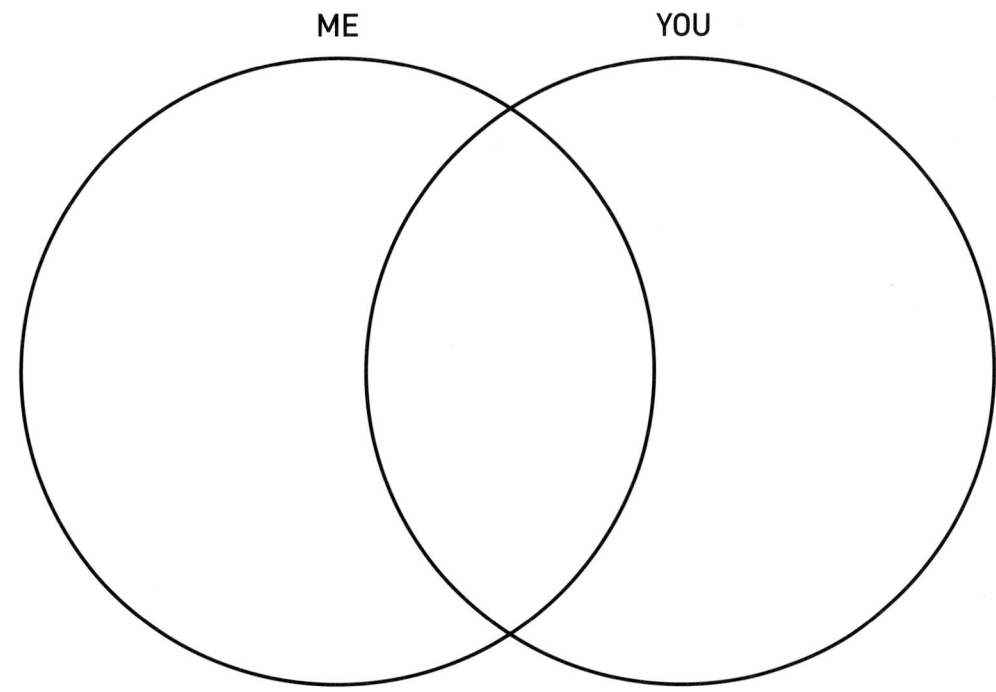

1-9 Pass & Score

Ice Breaker Activities

Type of activity
Group work / Ice breaker

Aim of activity
To talk about myself

Level
Beginner ~ pre-intermediate

Time
10 minutes

Target language
My favorite is ~ /
I want to ~ / My hobby is ~

How to do the activity

1. 학생들에게 27쪽의 worksheet을 나누어 줍니다. 제한시간 5분내로 worksheet에 있는 항목을 모두 채우도록 합니다.

2. 학생들을 2개의 팀으로 나눈 뒤 학생 한 명에게 공을 패스합니다. 공을 받은 학생은 자신이 작성한 worksheet을 보면서 교사가 주는 질문에 답을 해야 합니다. 공을 패스 받고 질문에 제대로 된 답을 하면 2점을 받습니다. 만일 공을 받은 학생이 대답을 잘 하지 못하면 공을 받은 점수 1점 밖에 획득하지 못합니다.

3. 한 팀의 학생에 대한 대답이 끝나면 이번에는 다른 팀의 학생에게 공을 패스하여 질문을 던집니다. 모든 학생들에게 기회를 주면 좋겠지만 ice breaker 활동이므로 5~7명 정도의 학생에게 공을 던지는 것이 좋습니다.

4. 만일 그 팀의 어느 누구도 공을 잡지 못하면 기회가 상대편에게 주어집니다.

Teacher's Talk

1. I'm going to give you a worksheet. I'll give you five minutes to write the basic information about yourself.

2. (After five minutes) Time's up. Put your pens down. Now, I'm going to divide you into two different teams and then toss this ball to one of you. When you catch the ball, you need to answer my question. You may look at your worksheet to answer the question. If you answer correctly, your team gets two points. If you cannot answer correctly, you get only one point for catching the ball. Also, if your team fails to catch the ball, the other team gets a chance to answer my question.

Ryan's Tip

1. 활동이 끝난 뒤 학생들이 작성한 worksheet을 수합하여 묶어 두면 student profile로 사용할 수 있습니다. 학생들에게 증명 사진을 하나씩 가지고 오도록 한 뒤 student profile에 붙여 두면 이름과 얼굴을 빨리 기억하는데 도움을 줄 수 있습니다. 맨 마지막에 있는 teacher's note에는 학생의 특징적인 사항을 쓰도록 합니다.

2. 활동에 이용하는 공은 천이나 고무 재질로 만든 것이어야 합니다. 유아용 문구점에서 쉽게 찾을 수 있습니다.

1-9 Pass & Score

------- [Fold Here] -------

Student Profile

Name :   Class :   Student # :

Birthday :   Nickname :

Phone Number :   Email :

Photo Here

(Favorites)

Favorite movie :   Favorite food :
Favorite subject :   Favorite animal :
Favorite color :   Favorite song :

(Family & Friends)

I have _____ family members.
I have (many / a few / few) **friends**.
Name of my best friends :

(Interests)

My hobby is _____.
On weekends, I like to _____.
I (like / don't like) **to study English**.

(Future Plans)

I want to go to this country :
I want to do this in the future (future job) :
I want to marry this kind of person (future wife / husband) :

(Teacher's Note)

1-10 Certificate & Award

Ice Breaker Activities

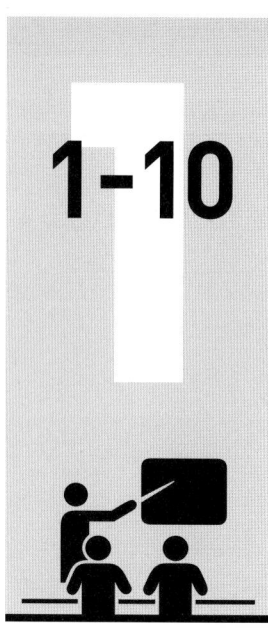

Type
Group work / Ice breaker

Aim
To present certificates and awards to students

Level
All level

Time
20 minutes

Language
Congratulations!
Excellent! Good Job!

How to do the activity

(Certificate)

1. 한 학기 수업이 다 끝나는 마지막 시간에 할 수 있는 활동입니다.

2. 학생들에게 수업을 성공적으로 마친 것에 대한 수료증을 증정하도록 합니다. 학생들을 한 명씩을 교실 앞으로 불러 상장을 수여하듯 증정하도록 합니다. 물론 비공식적인 수료증을 받는 것이지만 이 작은 종이 하나로 학생들은 작은 성취감을 느낄 수 있을 것입니다.

(Award - Shiny Star of the class)

1. 영어 과제를 성실히 수행한 학생, 각종 영어 활동을 하는데 있어서 두각을 보인 학생이나 큰 발전을 보인 학생들에게 수여하는 비공식적인 상이라고 할 수 있습니다.

2. Presented to 칸에는 학생의 이름을, For에는 학생이 참여한 활동 및 그 학생의 역할을, Date에는 날짜를, Presented by에는 교사의 이름과 서명을 쓰도록 합니다.

3. 상을 받은 학생들의 명단을 기록해 두면 추후에 생활기록부 '과목별 세부특기 사항'을 작성하는데 있어 편리하게 사용할 수 있습니다.

Teacher's Talk

1. This is the last English class of the semester. Before we finish the lesson today, I want to present you with a certificate for completing my English class. When I call your name, please come forward to get your certificate.

2. Thank you for everything that you have done in my class. I will not forget any of you. I'm not going to say "Good-bye" because we are going to meet again. Before I let you go, I want you to complete an evaluation of my class.

Ryan's Tip

1. 마지막 수업이 방학 이전에 있기 때문에 방학 때 학생들이 스스로 공부할 수 있도록 영어 추천 도서를 주시는 것도 잊지 마세요.

2. 선생님의 수업에 대한 학생들의 생각을 듣는 시간을 가지시는 것도 이 시간에 하실 수 있습니다. 무기명 설문지 방법을 이용하시면 되는데요. 맨 뒤(165쪽)에 제가 자주 쓰는 설문 양식을 실어두었습니다.

1-10 Certificate & Award

Certificate of Completion

This is to certify that _____ *successfully completed* _____*'s English class from* _____ *to* _____ .

_____
English Teacher

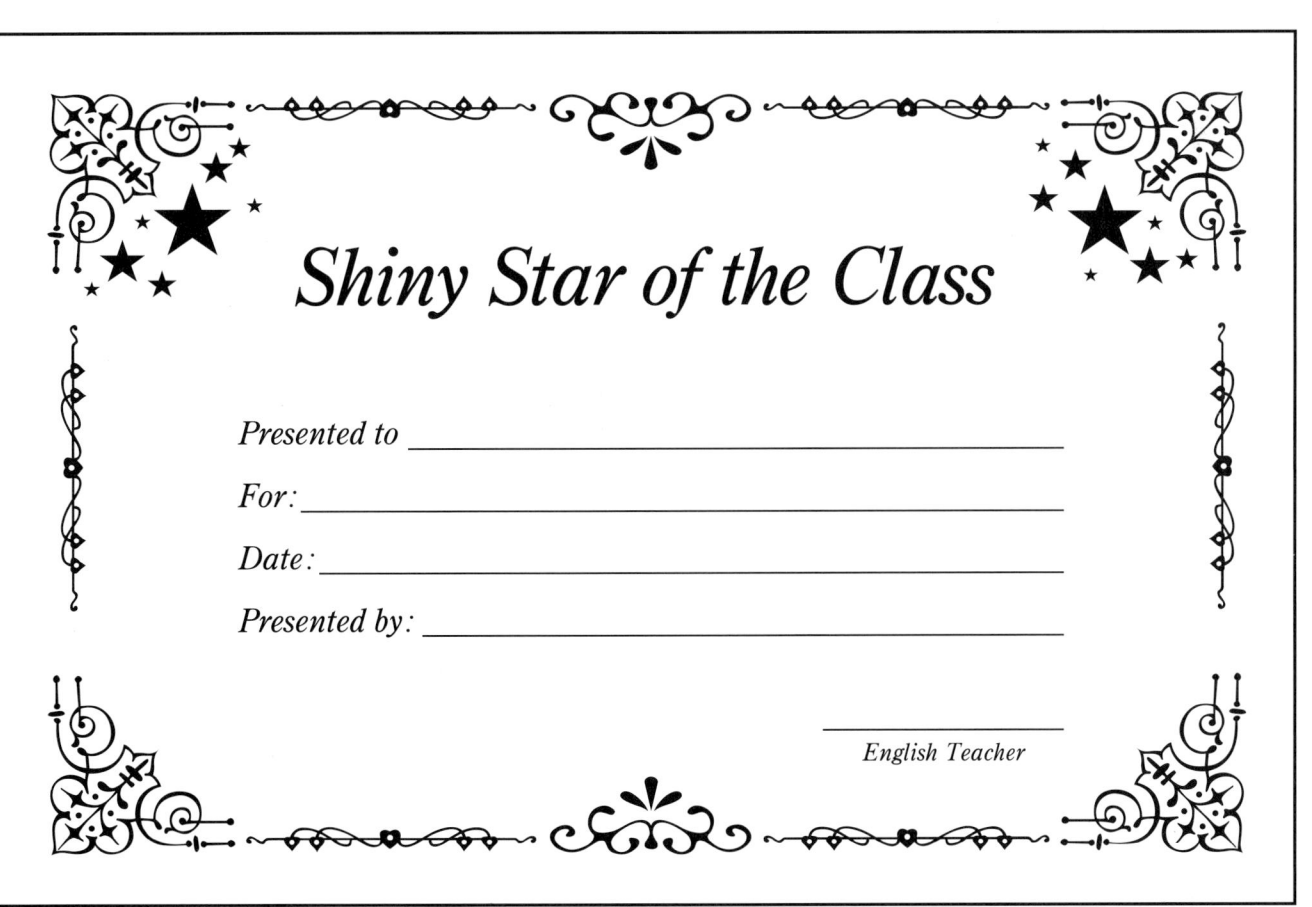

Shiny Star of the Class

Presented to _____

For: _____

Date: _____

Presented by: _____

_____
English Teacher

UNIT 2

Speaking
Activities

UNIT 2 Speaking Activities

2-1	Proverb Play (p.32 ~ p.35)
Type	Pair work
Aim	To make a short dialog using a proverb
Level	Pre-intermediate ~ intermediate
Time	50 minutes

2-2	Radio DJ (p.36 ~ p.37)
Type	Group work
Aim	To make suggestions for certain situations
Level	Pre-intermediate ~ intermediate
Time	50 minutes

2-3	Find the Spy (p.38 ~ p.41)
Type	Group work
Aim	To deliver a confidential message and then find the spy
Level	Beginner ~ pre-intermediate
Time	15 ~ 20 minutes

2-4	Me Card Game (p.42 ~ p.45)
Type	Pair work
Aim	To talk about myself
Level	Beginner
Time	50 minutes

2-5	Thank God, It's ~ (p.46 ~ p.47)
Type	Group work
Aim	To make a monthly calendar
Level	All level
Time	20 ~ 25 minutes

2-6	School Trip Interview (p.48 ~ p.53)
Type	Group work
Aim	To ask questions about the school trip
Level	Beginner ~ pre-intermediate
Time	25 ~ 30 minutes + assignment

2-7	Explore Korea (p.54 ~ p.57)
Type	Group work
Aim	To introduce Korean attractions
Level	Intermediate
Time	100 minutes (2 lessons)

2-8	Online Shopping for Christmas (p.58 ~ p.59)
Type	Pair work
Aim	To talk about Christmas presents / To buy presents online
Level	Beginner ~ pre-intermediate
Time	50 minutes

2-9	The Best Home Doctor (p.60 ~ p.63)
Type	Group work
Aim	To give medical advice
Level	Pre-intermediate
Time	50 minutes

2-10	The Die Story (p.64 ~ p.67)
Type	Group work
Aim	To create a story with pictures
Level	Intermediate
Time	100 minutes (2 lessons)

2-1 Proverb Play

Type
Pair work / Speaking

Aim
To make a short dialog using a proverb

Level
Pre-intermediate ~ intermediate

Time
50 minutes

Language
English proverbs

Speaking Activities

How to do the activity

(Find your other half)

1. 학생들을 세 분단으로 나눕니다. 각 분단에 10~12명의 학생들이 있습니다.
2. 33쪽의 여러 속담을 각 모둠 학생들의 숫자만큼 잘라 둡니다.
3. 학생들에게 미리 잘라 둔 속담의 반을 나누어 줍니다. 학생들은 자신이 받은 속담의 반을 암기한 후 주머니 속에 집어 넣습니다.
4. 학생들은 일어서서 자신의 속담의 나머지 반을 가진 학생을 찾아야 합니다. 반드시 자신의 모둠 안에서 나머지 반을 가지고 있는 학생을 찾습니다. 이 때 주머니 속에 있는 속담 종이를 꺼내 보여 주지 않도록 합니다. 학생들의 speaking을 좀 더 유도하고 속담을 암기하도록 하기 위함입니다.
5. 나머지 속담의 반을 찾았으면 두 학생이 짝이 되어 같이 앉도록 합니다.

(Make a dialog)

1. 학생들에게 34쪽의 sample dialog를 제시해 줍니다.
2. 자신의 속담을 사용하여 sample dialog과 유사한 대화를 만들도록 합니다. 두 명이 대사를 할 수 있는 dialog를 만들도록 합니다. 대사의 끝은 반드시 Just like the old saying, "_____" 로 끝내도록 합니다. dialog가 완성되면 10분 동안 파트너와 함께 대화를 연습하도록 합니다. 동작과 어조 등도 연습할 수 있도록 합니다.
3. 임의로 학생들을 선택하여 자신들이 제작한 proverb play를 다른 학생들 앞에서 연기합니다.

Teacher's Talk

1. First, I'm going to divide you into three different teams. Now, I'm going to give you half of a proverb. You need to memorize it and then put it in your pocket.
2. Next, you need to stand up and find the team member who has the other half of your proverb. You MUST NOT talk to the different teams. Also, you MUST NOT take the proverb out of your pocket. Just say your proverb. Once you find the right person, sit with him / her.
3. (Two minutes later) Let's check if you are sitting with the right person. Take out the half of your proverb.
4. Now, you and your partner need to make a short dialog using the proverb. Write your own dialog on the worksheet that I'm going to give you. You can refer to the sample dialog on the worksheet. I'll give you 20 minutes. Once you finish writing the dialog, practice the role play with your partner.

Ryan's Tip

1. 의외로 sample dialog를 만들고 연습하는데 시간이 많이 걸릴 수 있으므로 이 수업을 2차시로 진행할 수도 있습니다. 1차시에는 sample dialog를 만들고 연습할 수 있도록 하고, 2차시에는 연습했던 dialog를 모든 학생이 발표하도록 합니다.
2. 모든 학생들의 연극이 끝난 후 Proverb Play Award 시상식을 간단하게 진행하여 다음의 분야에 가장 뛰어난 학생들을 선정할 수도 있습니다.

Best Performance (최고 연기상) / Best Script (최고 대본상) / Best Preparation (최고 준비상)

2-1 Proverb Play

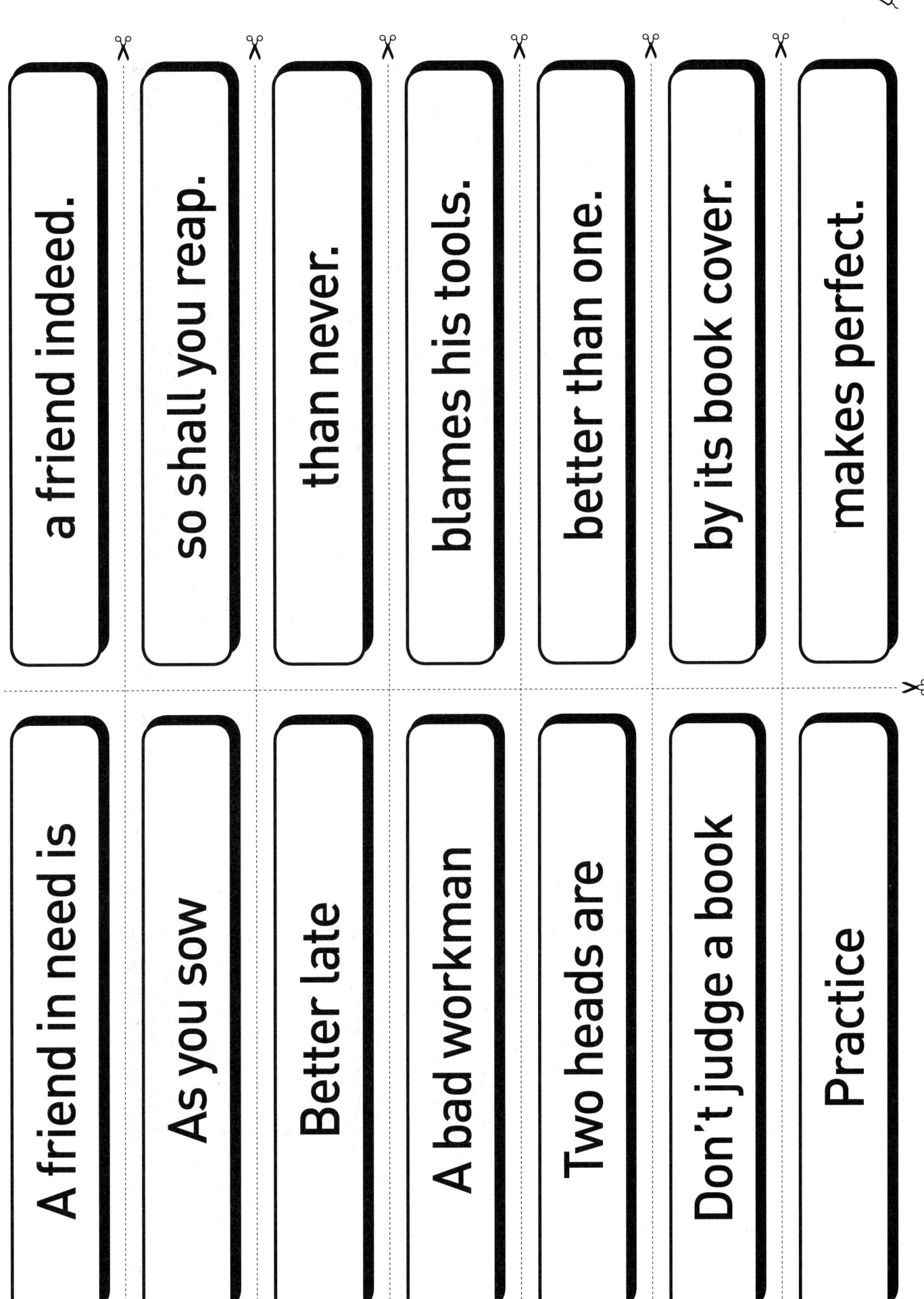

Speaking Activities

(Sample Dialog)

A : Hey, how did the game go last night?

B : Actually, we lost the game because of me.

A : Why? What happened?

B : I missed the last free throw. We could have won if I had made at least one shot.

A : It's okay. You'll do better next time.

B : I'm seriously thinking about quitting the team.

A : No way! Why don't you practice your free throws every day after school?

B : Do you think I can do better if I practice?

A : Absolutely! Just like the old saying, *"Practice makes perfect."*

Write your own dialog using your proverb.

A :

B :

A :

B :

A :

B :

A :

B :

A :

2-1 Proverb Play

Best Performance

Presented to _____

For: _____

Date: _____

Presented by: _____

_____
English Teacher

Best Script

Presented to _____

For: _____

Date: _____

Presented by: _____

_____
English Teacher

Best Preparation

Presented to _____

For: _____

Date: _____

Presented by: _____

_____
English Teacher

2-2 Radio DJ

Speaking Activities

Type
Group work / speaking

Aim
To make suggestions for certain situations

Level
Pre-intermediate ~ intermediate

Time
50 minutes

Language
Making suggestions (How about ~? / Why don't you~?) / Making proper comments for different situations

How to do the activity

1. 6명이 한 모둠을 만듭니다.
2. 각 모둠에 37쪽의 fan letter worksheet을 나누어 줍니다.
3. 각 모둠의 학생들은 9개의 fan letter 중 3개를 골라 그 상황에 맞는 멘트와 함께 가장 적절한 노래를 선정해 짧게 불러 주어야 합니다. 6명의 학생 중 3명의 학생이 상황에 맞는 멘트를, 그리고 나머지 3명의 학생이 가장 적절한 노래를 선정해 부르도록 임무를 분담합니다. 주어진 시간은 20분입니다.
4. 이제 라디오 쇼를 진행할 시간입니다. 멘트를 맡은 학생이 첫 번째 fan letter의 상황을 설명하고 모둠에서 정한 멘트를 읽어 줍니다. 그리고는 다른 학생들이 그에 가장 맞는 노래 한 곡을 10~20초간 짧게 부릅니다. 이렇게 해서 3개의 fan letter에 대한 멘트와 노래를 끝내면 다른 모둠이 나와서 라디오 쇼를 진행합니다.

Teacher's Talk

1. Today, you'll be the host of a famous radio show. First, I want you to make a group of six students. Now, I'm going to give you nine fan letters. Read them quickly and then choose only three fan letters that you want to talk about on your radio show.
2. Next, you need to make some comments or suggestions for the three fan letters. Also, you need to choose the most suitable song for each situation. Since you have six people in your group, three of you will make comments, and the other three will choose and sing the songs very briefly. It's just like a music talk show on the radio. I'll give you 20 minutes to prepare.
3. It's time to air the show. Group 1, come up and host your radio show. Tell us about your first fan letter and then give us your comments. After that, sing a song for your fans.

Ryan's Tip

1. 만일 50분내로 발표를 할 시간이 없다면 좀 더 준비를 완벽하게 해서 다음 시간에 라디오 쇼를 진행할 수 있도록 합니다.
2. 만일 group work가 여건상 힘들다면 pair work로 활동을 진행할 수 있습니다. 발표는 교사가 학생을 임의로 선정하여 하도록 합니다.

2-2 Radio DJ

I'm getting married today.
Your comment:
_____
_____

I have a newborn baby!
Your comment:
_____
_____

Today is my birthday.
Your comment:
_____
_____

My grandmother passed away.
Your comment:
_____
_____

I broke up with my girlfriend.
Your comment:
_____
_____

I failed the test.
Your comment:
_____
_____

Merry Christmas!
Your comment:
_____
_____

I feel worried about tomorrow's test.
Your comment:
_____
_____

I won the championship!
Your comment:
_____
_____

2-3

📣 Speaking Activities

Find the Spy

Type
Group work / Speaking

Aim
To deliver a confidential message and then find the spy

Level
Beginner ~ pre-intermediate

Time
15 ~ 20 minutes

Language
To describe physical appearances

How to do the activity

1. 5~6명이 한 줄로 앉도록 합니다. 보통 30명 이상의 학생이면 6줄이 바람직합니다.
2. 학생들은 FBI 요원이 되어 주어진 비밀 메시지에 따라 스파이를 찾아내야 합니다. 만일 스파이를 찾지 못하면 공항에서 폭탄이 터질 것입니다.
3. 각 줄의 맨 앞에 앉은 학생에게 39쪽에서 자른 confidential card를 하나씩 줍니다. 각 팀이 각각 다른 confidential card를 받습니다. 맨 뒤에 앉은 학생들에게는 40쪽에 있는 공항 그림을 줍니다. 맨 앞에 앉은 학생에게 1분을 주고 confidential card에 있는 스파이의 인상착의를 어떻게 영어로 설명할 지 생각하도록 합니다. 절대 confidential card를 다른 학생에게 보여 주어서는 안됩니다. 나머지 학생들은 책상에 엎드려 있습니다.
4. 교사가 "Find the spy!"라고 외치면 맨 앞 학생이 스파이의 인상착의를 두 번째 학생에게 귓속말로 이야기합니다. 전달이 끝나면 첫 번째 학생은 책상에 엎드립니다. 두 번째 학생은 세번째 학생에게 맨 앞 학생에게 들은 대로 스파이의 인상착의를 이야기 합니다. 이렇게 해서 맨 마지막 학생에게 메시지를 전달합니다. 맨 마지막 학생은 인상착의를 들은 대로 공항 그림에서 스파이를 찾아냅니다.
5. 마지막 학생들이 찾은 스파이와 첫 번째 학생이 가지고 있는 confidential card의 스파이가 일치하는지 확인합니다. 스파이가 일치하는 팀은 스파이를 잡아서 공항의 폭탄이 터지지 않지만, 일치하지 않는 팀은 폭탄이 터지게 되어 FBI 미션이 실패하게 됩니다. 다시 맨 앞에 앉은 학생에게 또 다른 confidential card를 주고 동일한 활동을 합니다. 3~4회 정도 활동을 하면 학생들이 describe하는데 익숙해 질 것입니다.

Teacher's Talk

1. (After putting six students in a row) Today, you're going to be FBI agents with a mission of finding a spy in the airport. If you fail this mission, the spy will detonate a bomb in the airport.
2. I'm going to give a "confidential card" to the first student in your row. Also, I'm going to give a "In the airport" picture to the last student in your row. The rest of you should cover your face with your hands. The confidential card has a picture of the spy. The first person should study the spy for a minute. When I say, "Find the Spy!" the first person describes the spy to the next person. You should whisper, not talk loud. Also, if you speak any Korean words, you have failed your mission.
3. When you finish delivering the message, the last person with the "In the airport" picture should say the name of the spy. If he/she says the right name, you save everyone in the airport. If not, the bomb will blow up the entire airport. Are you ready to find the spy? Let's do it!

Ryan's Tip

1. 인상착의를 전달하는데 시간을 정해두는 것이 좋습니다. 시간 내에 메시지를 전달하지 못하면 폭탄이 자동으로 터지게 된다고 말씀해 주세요.
2. 가장 중요한 것은 절대 한국어로 메시지를 전달하면 안 되는 것입니다. 그런 학생이 발견될 경우 자동으로 폭탄이 터지게 된다고 경고해 주세요.

2-3 Find the Spy

(Confidential Card)

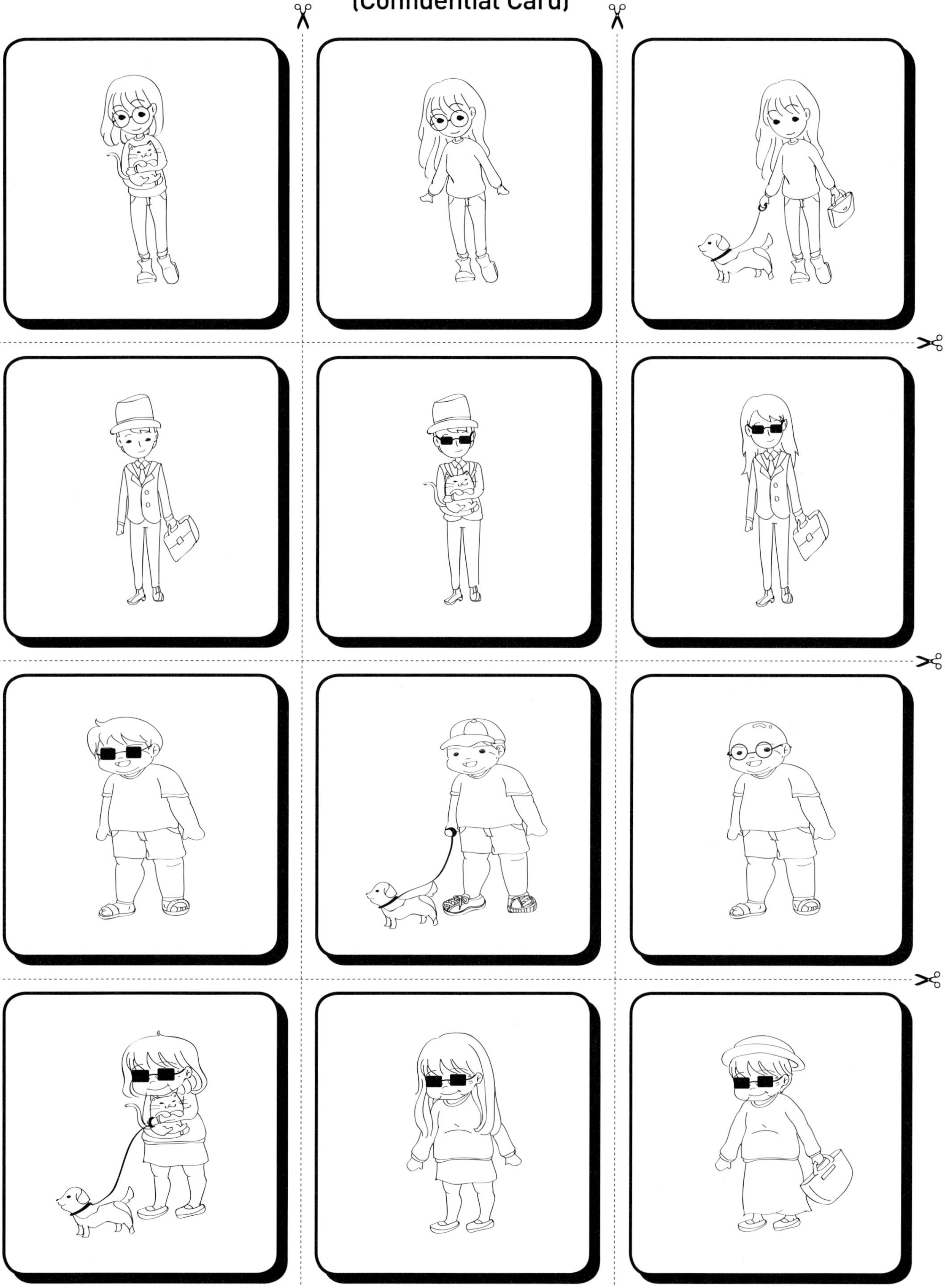

Speaking Activities

Find the spy in the airport

2-3 Find the Spy

Kim

Kelly

Dan

Ben

Susan

Gina

2-4

Speaking Activities

Me Card Game

Type
Pair work / Speaking

Aim
To talk about myself

Level
Beginner

Time
50 minutes

Language
I want to ~ / My favorite ~
I have ~ / I like to ~

How to do the activity

1. 짝과 함께 하는 활동입니다. 43쪽의 card를 잘라 학생들에게 나누어 줍니다. 학생들은 짝과 함께 각 질문에 해당하는 대답을 1분 만에 연결시켜야 합니다.
2. 연결활동이 끝나면 교사와 함께 질문과 대답에 대한 학습을 합니다.
3. 학습을 한 후 질문 카드를 모두 뒤집어 놓습니다. 대답 카드는 사용하지 않으므로 책상 한 쪽에 잘 모아 둡니다. 학생들은 질문 카드 하나를 뽑고 그 질문을 상대 학생에게 물어봅니다. 상대 학생은 교사와 함께 학습한 내용을 바탕으로 그 질문에 대답을 합니다. 대답을 마친 학생이 이번에는 질문 카드를 뽑고 상대방 학생에게 그 질문을 물어봅니다. 이런 방식으로 모든 질문 카드를 뽑아 묻고 대답하는 활동을 합니다.

Teacher's Talk

1. I'm going to give you two types of cards; one of them is a question card and the other one is an answer card. With your partner, you need to match the question cards with the correct answer cards. I'll give you one minute to match your cards.
2. Good Job! Let's check your answers now, shall we?
3. (After studying the questions and answers) Now, put away the answer cards and leave the question cards face down on the desk. Next, pick up a card and read the question to your partner. Your partner should answer the question. Take turns asking and answering the questions to each other.

Ryan's Tip

1. 이 활동을 writing activity로 발전시킬 수 있습니다. 이러한 guided writing activity는 영어 수준이 낮은 학생들에게 용이하게 사용할 수 있습니다.
2. 학생들에게 44쪽의 worksheet을 나누어 준 뒤 자신의 정보로 빈칸을 채우도록 합니다. worksheet은 앞서 진행한 speaking 활동의 질문과 대답을 그대로 옮겨 놓은 것입니다.
3. 학생들이 빈 칸을 모두 완성했으면 1번부터 16번까지의 문장을 45쪽의 writing worksheet에 적도록 합니다. 16번 문장 이후에 간략하게 2~3문장을 더 첨가하도록 합니다. 이렇게 하면 서론, 본론, 결론의 구조를 가진 자기 소개하는 글을 완성할 수 있습니다.

2-4 Me Card Game

What's your name?	1. My Name is **Sujin Park**.
How old are you?	2. I'm **17** years old.
Where were you born?	3. I was born in **Seoul**.
Where do you live?	4. I live in **Wolkye** dong. It's close to school.
What's your favorite book?	5. My favorite book is **Harry Potter**.
What's your favorite movie?	6. My favorite movie is **Superman**.
What sport do you enjoy?	7. I like **basketball**.
What kind of food do you like to eat?	8. I like to eat **pizza**.
Do you have food that you don't like to eat?	9. I don't like to eat **tofu**.
What school do you go to?	10. I go to **Yumkwang high school**. I'm in the **first** grade.
What's your favorite subject?	11. I like to study **English**.
What's the subject that you don't like to study?	12. I don't like to study **Math**.
Who is your favorite teacher?	13. I like **Mr. Jang Sok Kun**. He's **so kind and good-looking**.
Who is your best friend?	14. My best friend is **Jihye**. We like to **watch movies together**.
What's your hobby?	15. I like to **listen to music**.
What do you do on Sundays?	16. I **go to church**. Also, I **play computer games**.

 **Speaking Activities**

Fill in the blanks with your idea.

What's your name?	1. My Name is _____.
How old are you?	2. I'm _____ years old.
Where were you born?	3. I was born in _____.
Where do you live?	4. I live in _____.
What's your favorite book?	5. My favorite book is _____.
What's your favorite movie?	6. My favorite movie is _____.
What sport do you enjoy?	7. I like _____.
What kind of food do you like to eat?	8. I like to eat _____.
Do you have food that you don't like to eat?	9. I don't like to eat _____.
What school do you go to?	10. I go to _____. I'm in the _____ grade.
What's your favorite subject?	11. I like to study _____.
What's the subject that you don't like to study?	12. I don't like to study _____.
Who is your favorite teacher?	13. I like *Ms. / Mr.* _____. (S)He's _____.
Who is your best friend?	14. My best friend is _____. We like to _____.
What's your hobby?	15. I like to _____.
What do you do on Sundays?	16. I _____ on Sundays. Also, I _____.

2-4 Me Card Game

Using the sentences that you wrote, write a short passage to introduce yourself.

Name : _____ **Class :** _____ **Student Number :** _____

1. _____ 2. _____
_____ 3. _____
_____ 4. _____
_____ .

5. _____ 6. _____
_____ 7. _____
_____ 8. _____ 9. _____
_____ .

10. _____ 11. _____
_____ 12. _____
_____ 13. _____
_____ 14. _____
_____ .

15. _____ 16. _____
_____
_____
_____ .

This is who I am. I hope you know me better now. Thank you and have a good day.

2-5

Speaking Activities

Thank God, It's (month)!

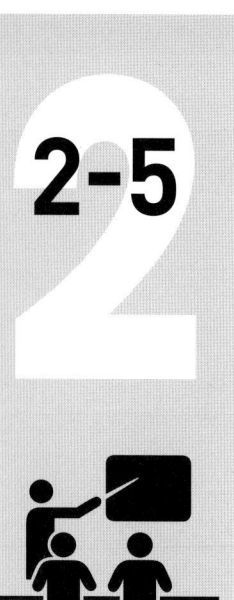

Type
Group work / speaking

Aim
To make a monthly calendar

Level
All level

Time
20 ~ 25 minutes

Language
1. Future tense (I'm going to / I'll)
2. Special events for the month

How to do the activity

1. 수업이 시작되기 전 미리 그 달에 있을 특별한 학교 행사와 날짜 혹은 그 달의 공휴일 등을 각각 조그만 쪽지에 적어 교실 벽이나 뒤에 붙여 놓습니다.
2. 47쪽의 달력에는 그 달의 날짜만 적고 학생 수대로 복사합니다.
3. 5~6명이 한 모둠이 됩니다. 각 모둠에서 runner 한 명을 선정합니다. runner는 수업시간에 참여를 잘 하지 않는 학생으로 선정해 주면 좋습니다.
4. runner는 벽에 붙은 그 달의 학교 행사 및 공휴일 등의 정보를 자신의 모둠 학생들에게 전달해야 합니다. 학생들은 runner가 전하는 그 달의 행사를 자신의 calendar에 적습니다.
5. 모둠 학생들 모두가 calendar를 채우면 "Thank God, It's (달 이름)!"을 외칩니다. 가장 빨리 구호를 외친 팀이 승리합니다.
6. 승리한 모둠이 monthly calendar에 적은 내용을 발표하도록 합니다. 발표를 통해서 교사가 이번 달에 어떤 행사가 있을지 정리해 주는 시간을 가집니다.

Teacher's Talk

1. Make a group of five students and choose a runner for your group.
2. If you look around the classroom, you'll see small pieces of paper on the wall. Those are the special events of the month. Your team runner will run to the wall, memorize the special events, and then return to your team to tell you the events. You need to write all the events on the calendar that I'm going to give you. Runner, you can go back and forth to the wall to deliver the message. However, you cannot write anything. You must memorize the events!
3. As soon as your team members finish filling up the calendar, you call, "Thank God, It's (this month)!" The team who calls out first wins the game.

Ryan's Tip

1. monthly calendar 작성이 끝나면 이번 달에 개인적으로 어떤 특별한 행사나 하고 싶은 일이 있는지 1분 동안 생각하도록 합니다. 가족, 친구 생일, 특별한 약속, 여행 계획, 공부 계획 등 구체적인 예를 제시해 주시면 좋습니다. 각자의 monthly calendar에 자신의 그 달 계획을 간단하게 쓰도록 합니다. monthly calendar 밑에는 자신의 개인적인 계획을 영어 문장으로 쓰도록 합니다. 문장을 완성하면 자신의 계획을 말해 보도록 합니다.

2-5 Thank God, It's (month)!

Mon	Tue	Wed	Thu	Fri	Sat	Sun

My special plans for this month

1. I'm going to _____
2. I'm going to _____
3. _____
4. _____

2-6 School Trip Interview

Type
Group work /
Speaking + Writing

Aim
To ask questions about
the school trip

Level
Beginner ~
pre-intermediate

Time
25 ~30 minutes +
Homework assignment

Language
Questions and answers
about the school trip

Speaking Activities

How to do the activity

1. 30명 이상의 수업일 경우 학생들을 3개의 분단으로 나눕니다. 인터뷰를 하기 위해 각 분단의 파트너들이 서로 마주보며 앉을 수 있도록 자리를 정렬합니다.

2. 각 분단의 왼쪽에 앉아 있는 학생들에게는 A, B, C, D, E, F의 인터뷰 용지를, 오른쪽에 앉아 있는 학생들에게는 G, H, I, J, K, L 의 인터뷰 용지를 나누어 줍니다.

3. 각 인터뷰 용지에 적힌 질문을 자신이 마주보며 앉은 파트너에게 서로 물어봅니다. 파트너의 이름과 대답을 인터뷰 용지에 기록합니다. 인터뷰 제한 시간은 1분 입니다.

4. 1분 뒤 왼쪽에 앉아 있는 학생들이 옆으로 한 칸씩 이동하도록 합니다. 맨 끝에 앉아 있는 학생은 맨 앞으로 이동합니다. 절대 오른쪽에 앉아 있는 학생은 이동하지 않습니다.

5. 똑같은 질문을 새로운 파트너에게 하고 이름과 대답을 인터뷰 용지에 적습니다. 1분의 제한 시간이 끝나면 왼쪽에 있는 학생이 다시 옆으로 이동합니다. 학생들이 상대편 줄의 학생들을 다 인터뷰할 때까지 (예를 들면 5줄로 구성된 분단이면 5명을 인터뷰 해야 함) 이 활동을 반복합니다.

6. 인터뷰가 끝난 뒤 자신의 인터뷰 용지를 살펴보고 가장 흥미로운 대답을 한 학생의 이름을 동그라미 치도록 합니다.

7. 각 분단의 2명씩을 지명해서 자신의 질문과 가장 흥미로운 대답을 읽도록 합니다.

8. 53쪽에 있는 "My School Trip to _____" 를 나눠 준 뒤 자신의 수학여행에 대한 짧은 기행문을 써 오도록 합니다.

Teacher's Talk

1. Students sitting in the left row will get a worksheet from A to F while students sitting in the right row will get a worksheet from G to L. There's a question on each worksheet. You're going to ask the question to your partner and then write his/her answer on the worksheet. One minute later, after asking each other the question, students sitting in the left row will move forward to the next seat while students in the right row remain seated. When you meet your new partner, you'll ask the same question and write down their answer. One minute later, students in the left row will move forward to the next seat again. You'll do this until you finish interviewing all the people in the opposite row.

2. (After the interview) Now, take a look at your worksheet and choose the most interesting answer.

3. Homework time. Based on the questions that you had today, think about your school trip, and write a short journal about the trip. Make sure you put a picture in your journal.

2-6 School Trip Interview

(A) Ask the following question to your friends and then write their answers in the chart.

Question : What did you pack in your luggage?	
Friend's name	Answer

✂ -

(B) Ask the following question to your friends and then write their answers in the chart.

Question : How did you feel before the school trip?	
Friend's name	Answer

✂ -

(C) Ask the following question to your friends and then write their answers in the chart.

Question : What did you do on the bus?	
Friend's name	Answer

라이언 쌤, 이렇게 가르쳐서 영어수업 대박내다 Ⅱ - **활동편**

Speaking Activities

(D) Ask the following question to your friends and then write their answers in the chart.

Question : What was your most exciting experience during the school trip?	
Friend's name	Answer

(E) Ask the following question to your friends and then write their answers in the chart.

Question : What was your least exciting experience during the school trip?	
Friend's name	Answer

(F) Ask the following question to your friends and then write their answers in the chart.

What did you buy for a souvenir?	*souvenir : 기념품
Friend's name	Answer

2-6 School Trip Interview

(G) Ask the following question to your friends and then write their answers in the chart.

Question : How was your room? Did you sleep well at night?	
Friend's name	Answer

(H) Ask the following question to your friends and then write their answers in the chart.

Question : What was your most memorable experience on the first day?	
Friend's name	Answer

(I) Ask the following question to your friends and then write their answers in the chart.

Question : What was your most memorable experience on the second day?	
Friend's name	Answer

Speaking Activities

(J) Ask the following question to your friends and then write their answers in the chart.

Question : How was the food during the school trip? What was your favorite food?	
Friend's name	Answer

(K) Ask the following question to your friends and then write their answers in the chart.

Question : Did you take many pictures? Whom did you take the best picture with?	
Friend's name	Answer

(L) Ask the following question to your friends and then write their answers in the chart.

Question : How did you feel when you got home?	
Friend's name	Answer

2-6 School Trip Interview

My School Trip to _____

Class :　　　　　**Student # :**　　　　　**Name :**

(Stage I : Think about the answers for the following questions)

1. What did you pack in your luggage?
2. How did you feel before the school trip?
3. What did you do on the bus?
4. What was your most exciting experience during the school trip?
5. What was your least exciting experience during the school trip?
6. What did you buy for a souvenir?
7. How was your room? Did you sleep well at night?
8. What was your most memorable experience on the first day?
9. What was your most memorable experience on the second day?
10. How was the food during the school trip? What was your favorite food?
11. Did you take many pictures? Whom did you take the best picture with?
12. How did you feel when you got home?

(Stage II : Based on the answers above, write a short essay about your school trip.)

_____
_____
_____
_____
_____
_____
_____
_____
_____
_____
_____
_____

 Speaking Activities

2-7 Explore Korea

Type
Group Work / Speaking

Aim
To introduce Korean attractions

Level
Intermediate

Time
50 minutes (brainstorming) + 50 minutes (presentation)

Language
Take a bus ~ /
It opens at ~ /
You need to pay ~

How to do the activity

1. 원어민 교사와의 협력 수업 시 사용할 수 있는 활동입니다.

2. 학생들을 6개의 모둠으로 나눕니다. 55~57쪽에 있는 한국에 관한 6가지의 주제를 보여 준 뒤 각 모둠에서 한 가지 주제를 선택하도록 합니다.

3. 각 학교에 소속된 원어민 교사가 한국을 직접 체험할 수 있도록 학생들은 자신의 주제에 맞게 구체적인 계획을 세워야 합니다. 학생들이 해야 할 가장 첫 번째 일은 각 주제에 맞게 어떤 곳을 갈 것인지 선정하는 것입니다. 그리고 그 장소를 선정한 이유, 그 곳에서 해야 할 일, 교통편, 이용 시간, 요금 등의 구체적인 정보도 제시합니다. 미리 학생들에게 원어민 교사가 사는 곳의 위치나 음식의 선호도, 취미 등의 정보를 이야기 해 주면 학생들이 계획을 수립하는데 도움을 줄 수 있습니다.

4. 다음 차시에서 발표를 진행합니다. 발표가 시작되기 전 원어민 교사에게 각 모둠에서 작성한 55~57쪽의 worksheet을 전달합니다. 그리고 발표에 관련된 심사나 심사평을 원어민 교사가 할 수 있도록 합니다.

Teacher's Talk

1. Mr. Bourne really wants to experience Korean culture, but he doesn't know where to start. So, today we're going to help him experience the real Korea by doing this activity.

2. First of all, I'm going to show you six different cultural experiences in Korea. What you need to do in your group is to decide which experience you are going to introduce to Mr. Bourne.

3. Now, I'm going to give you a worksheet. You need to decide which place would be best for him to visit. After that, you should talk about why he should go there, how he can get there, admission, etc. You're going to give a brief presentation to Mr. Bourne during the next class.

4. In order to help you to plan his excursion, Mr. Bourne will tell you about himself such as where he lives, what he likes to eat, what he can't eat, and so on.

Ryan's Tip

1. 원어민의 참여가 반드시 요구되는 활동이므로 수업 전에 미리 원어민의 역할과 한국 교사의 역할에 대해서 충분한 사전 협의가 있어야 합니다.

2-7 Explore Korea

Theater Performance	
Where to go	
Reasons of visiting	
How to get there	
Hour	
Admission	
Other information	

✂ -

Historical Place	
Where to go	
Reasons of visiting	
How to get there	
Hour	
Admission	
Other information	

Speaking Activities

Food	
Where to go	
Special menu	
How to get there	
Hour	
Price	
Other information	

Museum	
Where to go	
What to do	
How to get there	
Hour	
Admission	
Other information	

2-7 Explore Korea

Shopping	
Where to go	
What to buy	
How to get there	
Hour	
Special Sale	
Other information	

Young Culture	
Where to go	
What to do	
How to get there	
Hour	
Admission	
Other information	

2-8 Online Shopping for Christmas

Speaking Activities

Type
Pair work / Speaking + reading

Aim
To talk about Christmas presents / To buy presents online

Level
Beginner ~ pre-intermediate

Time
50 minutes

Language
The best presents that I've ever received
I'm going to buy ~

How to do the activity

1. 이 활동은 인터넷을 이용한 활동이므로 컴퓨터 실에서 이루어지는 것이 좋습니다.
2. 학생들 각자에게 59쪽의 worksheet을 나누어 줍니다.
3. ⟨A⟩ 활동에서 자신이 받은 가장 좋은 크리스마스 선물이 무엇이었는지 표를 작성하고 짝과 함께 비교해 보도록 합니다. ⟨B⟩ 활동에서 이번 크리스마스에 누구에게 무슨 선물을 사 줄 지를 생각하고 표를 작성하도록 합니다.
4. ⟨C⟩ 활동은 ⟨B⟩번에서 생각한 크리스마스 선물을 인터넷으로 구입하는 활동입니다. 학생들은 해외 인기있는 온라인 쇼핑몰 www.macys.com과 www.amazon.com 등을 이용하여 자신이 원하는 물건을 선택하고 그 정보를 표에 적습니다. 물건을 구입할 수 있는 학생들의 전체 예산은 $500로 한정되어 있습니다.
5. 표 작성이 끝나면 짝과 함께 자신이 가상으로 구입한 물품의 목록을 비교해 보도록 합니다.

Teacher's Talk

1. Today, you're going to buy Christmas presents for your friends and family. Before you go shopping, I want you to think about the best presents that you've ever received on Christmas and then complete the chart on the worksheet.
2. (Two minutes later) Now, let's talk about your best Christmas presents with your partner.
3. What do you want to buy for your family and friends this Christmas? Fill in the chart on the worksheet.
4. Now, it's time to go shopping! You have $500 to buy Christmas presents for your loved ones. Turn on your computer and go to the following online shopping websites to find the best presents. For each gift you buy, write down the price and description in the chart. I'll give you 20 minutes for online shopping.
5. (20 minutes later) Okay, everyone, let's share your shopping list with your partner.

Ryan's Tip

1. 한국 인터넷 사이트에서 쇼핑목록을 작성하지 않도록 합니다. 이 수업의 목표 중의 하나는 인터넷을 이용한 reading (scanning) skill 향상입니다.
2. 수업이 끝난 후 ⟨C⟩번 부분만 수합하여 크리스마스 때까지 교실 뒤 게시판이나 복도에 게시해 두면 크리스마스 분위기를 연출할 수 있습니다.

2-8 Online Shopping for Christmas

Merry Christmas 🎁

A. What are the best Christmas presents that you've ever received? Fill in the chart.

When	Present	From Whom
last year	a brand-new cell phone	My sister

B. What present are you going to give to the following people this Christmas?

To whom	Present
eg) my mom	a nice hat
my mom	
my dad	
my friend_____	

C. You have $500 to buy presents for your loved ones. Go to the following online shopping malls and find the best Christmas presents. Make sure to fill in the chart while you're shopping.
website : www.amazon.com / www.macys.com / www.nordstrom.com

(_____'s Christmas Shopping List)

To whom	Present	Price	Description including brand name
my mom	a nice hat	$28	Nine West Hat, Wool Newsboy Metal buckle along brim (gray color)

2-9

The Best Home Doctor

Speaking Activities

Type
Group work / Speaking

Aim
To give medical advice

Level
Pre-intermediate

Time
50 minutes

Language
Making suggestion
(You should ~ /
Why don't you ~ /
You'd better ~)

How to do the activity

학생들에게 우리가 일상 생활에서 흔히 볼 수 있는 질병들이 무엇인지 물어봅니다. 그 후 62~63 쪽에 등장하는 10가지 sickness들을 제시하고 병원에 가기 전에 집에서 할 수 있는 간단한 치료 법은 어떤 것이 있는지 이야기 해 봅니다. 이 단계에서는 학생들의 의견을 들을 뿐 정답을 제시하지 않습니다.

1. 학생들 모두에게 61쪽의 Home Doctor's Remedies를 나누어 줍니다. 학생들과 같이 worksheet을 보면서 집안에서 할 수 있는 치료법들을 간단하게 설명합니다.

2. 이제 본격적으로 The Best Home Doctor 활동을 진행합니다. 학생 4명이 한 모둠을 만들고 4명 중 한 명이 patient 역할을 나머지 3명이 home doctor 역할을 하도록 합니다. patient 역할을 맡은 학생이 62~63쪽의 sickness 카드 하나를 다른 3명의 의사들에게 제시하면 그에 맞는 적절한 remedy를 가장 빨리 제시한 의사가 그 카드를 소유할 수 있습니다. 가장 많은 sickness 카드를 소유한 의사가 그 모둠의 the best home doctor가 됩니다. patient는 remedy worksheet을 보면서 학생들이 정답을 이야기하고 있는지 확인합니다. 문장을 완벽하게 이야기 하지 않아도 됩니다. 영어 수준이 낮은 학생들의 경우 굵은 글씨로 되어 있는 핵심 단어만 이야기 해도 정답으로 인정합니다.

3. 활동을 진행하기 전에 의사들이 Home Doctor's Remedies 차트를 숙지할 수 있는 시간을 약 5분 정도 주도록 합니다. 굵은 글씨로 되어 있는 핵심단어를 중심으로 학습하도록 합니다. 게임 진행 시 patient는 "I have_____(병명)." 을, 의사들은 "You should_____(조언)." "Why don't you_____?" 와 같은 target language를 사용하도록 합니다.

Teacher's Talk

1. Can you name some common sicknesses and injuries that you may get in life? (Students answer. Teacher writes their answers on the board.) Now, can you tell me how to cure them at home?

2. Here are ten common sicknesses and injuries (from p.62~63). I'm going to give you Home Doctor's Remedies. Let's take a look at how to cure them at home.

3. Now, we're going to play a game. I want you to make groups of four students. One of you should be the patient and the rest of you should be doctors.

4. The patient will show a sickness card saying, "Doctors, I have _____." The doctor who gives the proper remedy first gets the sickness card. When you say the remedy, you should use expressions like "You should_____." or "Why don't you _____?" At the end of the game, the doctor who collects the most sickness cards will be the best home doctor.

5. Now, I'm going to give you five minutes for the doctors to study Home Doctor's Remedies chart. Patient, come here and get the sickness cards from me.

(Home Doctor's Remedies)

*Before you go see a doctor, you can do the following things at home.

Headache : Rub a few drops of ***aroma oil*** on your temples.
Sprained ankle : Put ***a bag of ice*** on your ankle. Keep your ankle elevated.
Fever : Drink ***plenty of water*** to reduce your body temperature.
Sore throat : Gargle with warm ***salt water***. Also, drink lots of water or juice.
Cold : Stay warm and ***rest in bed***. Also, drink hot tea such as ginger tea.
Upset stomach : Stay away from soda drinks. Add ***a spoon of honey*** in your tea.
Insect bite : Do not scratch the bite area. Put some ***toothpaste or mud*** on the bite.
Burn : Cool the burned area with ***cold running water*** if the burn is not serious.
Bloody nose : Do not tilt your head back. ***Lean forward*** to let the blood come out of your nose.
Rash : Avoid scrubbing your skin. ***Baking soda*** can be helpful to ease the itching.

remedy 치료법 / rub 문지르다 / temple 관자놀이 / sprained 접지른 (삔) / elevate 올리다 / reduce 줄이다 / gargle 입 안을 헹구다 / ginger 생강 / upset stomach 소화불량 / stay away from ~를 하지 않다 / scratch 긁다 / tilt (뒤로) 젖히다 / forward 앞으로 / rash 발진 / scrub 문지르다 (긁다) / ease 덜어주다 / itching 가려움

(Home Doctor's Remedies)

*Before you go see a doctor, you can do the following things at home.

Headache : Rub a few drops of ***aroma oil*** on your temples.
Sprained ankle : Put ***a bag of ice*** on your ankle. Keep your ankle elevated.
Fever : Drink ***plenty of water*** to reduce your body temperature.
Sore throat : Gargle with warm ***salt water***. Also, drink lots of water or juice.
Cold : Stay warm and ***rest in bed***. Also, drink hot tea such as ginger tea.
Upset stomach : Stay away from soda drinks. Add ***a spoon of honey*** in your tea.
Insect bite : Do not scratch the bite area. Put some ***toothpaste or mud*** on the bite.
Burn : Cool the burned area with ***cold running water*** if the burn is not serious.
Bloody nose : Do not tilt your head back. ***Lean forward*** to let the blood come out of your nose.
Rash : Avoid scrubbing your skin. ***Baking soda*** can be helpful to ease the itching.

remedy 치료법 / rub 문지르다 / temple 관자놀이 / sprained 접지른 (삔) / elevate 올리다 / reduce 줄이다 / gargle 입 안을 헹구다 / ginger 생강 / upset stomach 소화불량 / stay away from ~를 하지 않다 / scratch 긁다 / tilt (뒤로) 젖히다 / forward 앞으로 / rash 발진 / scrub 문지르다 (긁다) / ease 덜어주다 / itching 가려움

🎤 Speaking Activities

headache

sprained ankle

fever

sore throat

cold

2-9 The Best Home Doctor

2-10 The Die Story

Speaking Activities

Type
Group work / Speaking

Aim
To create a story with pictures

Level
Intermediate

Time
50 minutes (story making) + 50minutes (presentation)

Language
Storytelling

How to do the activity

1. 4명의 학생이 한 모둠이 되도록 합니다. 각 조의 학생들에게 65쪽과 66쪽에 있는 그림판을 양면 복사하여 나누어 줍니다. 또한 각 조에 주사위 하나씩도 나누어 줍니다. 67쪽의 스토리 보드는 모든 학생들이 하나씩 받도록 합니다.

2. 그림판은 10개의 항목으로 구성되어 있으며 각 항목에는 6개의 그림이 그려져 있습니다. 각 그림의 왼쪽 코너에는 1~6까지의 숫자가 적혀 있는데 학생들이 주사위를 던져 나오는 숫자대로 그림을 선택하게 됩니다. 총 10개의 항목이므로 주사위를 던져서 10개의 그림을 선택하게 되는 것입니다.

3. 학생들은 선택된 10개의 그림으로 하나의 스토리를 만들어야 합니다. 각자 받은 스토리 보드에 우선 자신이 배정 받은 10개의 항목을 씁니다. 그리고 그 그림들을 이용하여 하나의 스토리를 만들도록 합니다. 10개의 그림을 모두 사용하는 것이 원칙이나 1, 2개 정도는 사용하지 않아도 좋습니다.

4. 스토리가 완성되었으면 다음시간에 그 모둠 내에서 각자 자신의 스토리를 발표하도록 합니다.

Teacher's Talk

1. Let's make groups of four students. I'm going to give you a picture worksheet. Also, each one of you will receive a storyboard where you can create your own story. Now, I'll tell you how to make a story.

2. First of all, there are ten sections on the worksheet such as character, place, vehicle, etc. Each section has six different elements, and they have a number from 1 to 6 on the left top corner. Roll a die, and the element of the number on the die is yours. For example, if you roll a "five" on the main character section, your main character is Dan, a teenage boy. By rolling the die, you can choose ten key elements that you can use to make a story.

3. Write down all the key elements on your storyboard to create your story. You should try to use all the key elements; however, you can take out one or two elements, if necessary.

4. (Next class) It's time to present your story to your group members. Before telling your story, you need to mention what elements you chose in the previous class.

Ryan's Tip

1. 영어 수업 시간에 학생 중심의 활동을 하는데 있어서 반드시 필요한 물품들입니다. 언제 갑자기 쓸 수 있으니 반드시 학생들 수 대로 혹은 학생들의 모둠 수대로 준비해 주시면 좋습니다.

(1) 주사위   (2) 풀 / 가위   (3) 색연필 / 크레파스   (4) A4 / B4 색지

The Die Story

Roll a die and circle the number of each picture.

(Character)

(Personality)

(Place)

(Things)

(Vehicle)

🎤 Speaking Activities

(Animal)

| cat | ant | eagle | snake | bear | shark |

(Food & Drink)

| pizza | Kimchi | steak | hamburger | fish | no food |

(Weapon)

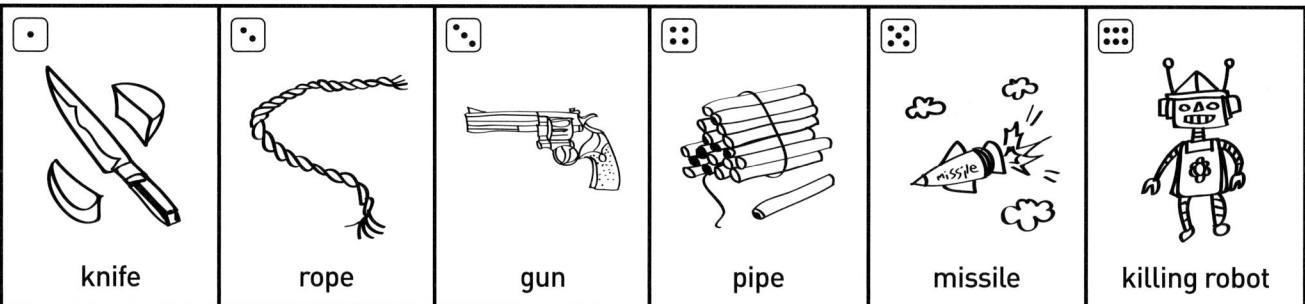

| knife | rope | gun | pipe | missile | killing robot |

(Event)

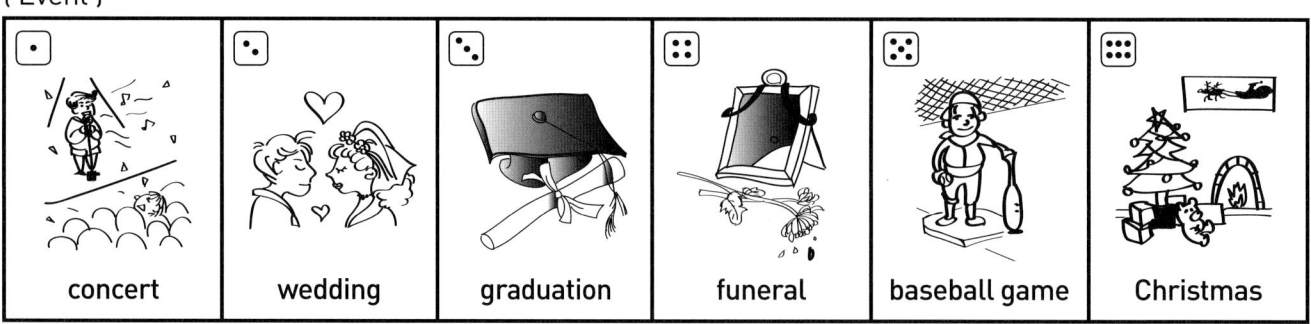

| concert | wedding | graduation | funeral | baseball game | Christmas |

(Natural Disaster)

| drought | snowstorm | hurricane | tsunami | earthquake | flood |

2-10 The Die Story

(_____'s storyboard)

Key Elements	* * * * * * * * * *
My Story	

UNIT 3

Writing
Activities

UNIT 3 Writing Activities

3-1	Text Messages on Special Days (p.70 ~ p.71)
Type	Solo work
Aim	To send text messages on special days
Level	All level
Time	15 minutes

3-2	Postcard from My Imaginary Vacation (p.72 ~ p.77)
Type	Solo work
Aim	To write a postcard
Level	Intermediate
Time	30 minutes + assignment

3-3	Describe the Masterpiece Painting (p.78 ~ p.79)
Type	Solo work
Aim	To write a short paragraph about a painting
Level	Pre-intermediate ~ intermediate
Time	30 minutes

3-4	Life Is Full of Choices (p.80 ~ p.85)
Type	Solo work
Aim	To write a short story in a guided activity
Level	Pre-intermediate
Time	50 minutes

3-5	My Favorite TV Show (p.86 ~ p.87)
Type	Solo work
Aim	To write about their favorite TV shows
Level	Pre-intermediate
Time	30 minutes + assignment

3-6	My Chart (p.88 ~ p.89)
Type	Solo work
Aim	To write sentences using student's own charts
Level	Pre-intermediate
Time	40 minutes

3-7	Describe This Job (p.90 ~ p.91)
Type	Group work
Aim	To describe jobs
Level	Beginner ~ pre-intermediate
Time	10 ~ 15 minutes

3-8	Create Your Future Resume (p.92 ~ p.93)
Type	Solo work
Aim	To write a resume
Level	Pre-intermediate ~ intermediate
Time	40 minutes + assignment

3-9	Plan Your Date (p.94 ~ p.97)
Type	Solo work
Aim	To plan an imaginary date
Level	Intermediate
Time	50 minutes

3-10	Publish the School Newspaper (p.98 ~ p.99)
Type	Group work
Aim	To make a school newspaper
Level	Intermediate
Time	100 minutes (2 lessons)

3-1

✏️ **Writing Activities**

Text Messages on Special Days

Type
Solo work / Writing

Aim
To send text messages on special days

Level
All level

Time
15 minutes

Language
Short text messages

How to do the activity

1. 스승의 날, 어버이 날, 크리스마스, 발렌타인 데이 등 특별한 날에 수업이 있을 경우 사용할 수 있는 활동입니다.

2. 학생들 각자에게 71쪽의 worksheet을 나누어 줍니다. 특별한 날 메시지 중에서 자신이 좋아하는 것을 하나 고릅니다.

3. 자신이 선택한 메시지를 하단에 있는 핸드폰 스크린에 적습니다. 그리고 자신만의 짧은 메시지를 영어로 덧붙이도록 합니다. 마지막으로 보내는 사람의 이름(전화번호)을 핸드폰 옆에 쓰도록 합니다.

Teacher's Talk

1. Today is Parents' Day. Did you buy some presents for your parents? Did you write a card for them? If you didn't do anything yet, I will give you a chance to send a lovely message to your parents from class today.

2. I'm going to give you a worksheet. You'll see a few messages that people commonly use on special occasions. Choose only one message that best describes your feelings for your parents and then write it on the cell phone screen. Make sure you add your own personal message at the end. Lastly, write the names of your recipients or their cell phone numbers.

3. If you have any questions, don't hesitate to raise your hand.

Ryan's Tip

1. 수업이 끝나고 쉬는 시간에 학생들이 직접 핸드폰을 이용하여 메시지를 보내도록 하는 것이 좋습니다.

2. 71쪽의 handout을 계속 학생들이 보관하도록 했다가 특별한 날이 다가오면 수업시간에 Icebreaker 활동으로 사용할 수 있습니다.

3. 특별한 날을 위한 E-card 보내기 활동도 할 수 있습니다. 인터넷에는 무료 E-card 웹사이트가 많이 있는데요. 그 중 한 사이트에서 자신이 원하는 카드를 골라 메시지를 영어로 쓴 뒤 다른 학생들이나 부모님의 이메일로 전송하는 활동입니다. 물론 모든 학생들이 컴퓨터를 사용할 수 있는 공간을 확보하는 것이 필수입니다.

3-1 Text Messages on Special Days

Text Messages on Special Days

Teachers' Day

- ☐ Thank you for guiding me and inspiring me with your lessons.
- ☐ Thank you so much for all the things you have done for me.
- ☐ You make me what I am today. Thank you so much. Happy Teacher's Day.
- ☐ It's your day, Ms. XXX. Happy Teacher's Day.
- ☐ I'm so lucky to have a wonderful teacher like you. Thank you so much.

Parents' Day

- ☐ Mom & Dad, you will never know how much I love you. Thank you so much.
- ☐ You're the best part of my life. Happy Parent's Day.
- ☐ Thank you for putting up with me all the time. I love you, mom & dad.
- ☐ You're the best parents in the world. I'll try to be the best son (daughter) to you too.
- ☐ I'm so blessed to have special parents like you.

Christmas

- ☐ May this Christmas bring joy and happiness to your family.
- ☐ May the miracle of Christmas fill your heart with joy and happiness.
- ☐ All I want for Christmas is you and your love. Merry Christmas.
- ☐ I hope you can enjoy the Christmas spirit with your family.
- ☐ May the grace of the Holy Father be with you and your family.

Valentine's Day

- ☐ I don't need chocolate. All I want today is your sweet love.
- ☐ Will you give me the honor of being your Valentine?
- ☐ You make my heart continue to beat. Happy Valentine's Day.
- ☐ I just want the world to know that you're my Valentine.
- ☐ You mean the world to me. Happy Valentine's Day.

To: _____
(number:)

From: _____
(Your name:)

라이언 쌤, 이렇게 가르쳐서 영어수업 대박내다 II - **활동편**

3-2 Postcard from My Imaginary Vacation

✏️ **Writing Activities**

Type
Solo work / Writing

Aim
To write a postcard

Level
Intermediate

Time
15 minutes (1st lesson) +
Homework assignment +
20 minutes (2nd lesson)

Language
visited / walked / ate /
met / saw / stayed / did /
rode / toured / bought

How to do the activity

1. 학생들에게 73쪽의 sample postcard를 잘라서 나누어 줍니다. 학생들이 sample postcard를 읽고 다음의 질문에 답하도록 합니다.

(Question 1) Where did Sarah go for vacation?
(Question 2) What places did she visit in Sydney?
(Question 3) What did she see in the garden?
(Question 4) Who did she meet on the second day?

2. 학생들에게 New York / London / Tokyo / Egypt / Paris / Africa / Jeju do / Alaska의 8곳을 제시해 주고 자신이 3일 동안 방문하고 싶은 장소를 1곳만 정하도록 합니다. 그 후 그 장소에 맞는 postcard를 74~77쪽에서 복사하여 각 학생들에게 나누어 줍니다.

3. 학생들은 3일 동안 그 장소로 여행을 한다고 가정을 하고 반 친구 한 명에게 자신이 한 일을 postcard에 적도록 합니다. 이 때 postcard에 제시된 10가지 동사 중 5가지 이상을 사용해야 합니다. 자신의 여행지에 대한 구체적인 정보를 얻기 위해 인터넷 등의 자료를 이용하도록 합니다.

4. 두 번째 수업 시간에 학생들은 자신이 작성한 postcard를 다른 학생에게 직접 전달합니다. 학생들에게 postcard를 읽을 시간을 준 뒤 교사는 위와 유사한 질문을 던집니다.

Teacher's Talk

1. I'm going to give you a postcard that my best friend, Sarah, sent to me a year ago. I'll give you two minutes to read the postcard, and answer the questions. Here are the questions.

2. (After concept checking) New York, London, Tokyo, Egypt, Paris, Africa, Jeju do and Alaska. Among these places, you have to choose only one place to visit for three days.

3. Now, I'm going to give you a postcard of each place. Your homework is to do some research on one of the places. You can check some travel websites to find out where to visit, what to eat, where to stay, and what to do there. Using the information from your research, you should write a postcard. Choose a friend in class that you want to send the card to. If you look at the top of the postcard, you will see 10 action words. Use at least 5~7 words to describe what you do there.

4. (Next Class) Okay, deliver your postcard to your friend.

5. Read your friend's postcard. Now, I'm going to ask you some questions about your friend's postcard. Kisu, Who sent you the postcard? Where did he/she visit?

3-2 Postcard from My Imaginary Vacation

Sydney is a fascinating place. Soon after arriving at the airport, I visited the Opera House. It was smaller than I expected. I bought this postcard at the Opera House. I ate Fish & Chips at a restaurant called DOV and then walked to the pier. I rode a ferry to Darling Harbor where I stayed my first night.

On the second day, I toured the national museum. I took a lot of photos in the museum. In the garden of the museum, I saw kangaroos hopping around. For dinner, I met my uncle, who has lived in Auburn for 10 years. After dinner, we went to the musical, Wicked. I had a great time with him.
I hope this postcard finds you well. See you later back in school.

To : Ryan Park

From : Sarah Jung

Sydney is a fascinating place. Soon after arriving at the airport, I visited the Opera House. It was smaller than I expected. I bought this postcard at the Opera House. I ate Fish & Chips at a restaurant called DOV and then walked to the pier. I rode a ferry to Darling Harbor where I stayed my first night.

On the second day, I toured the national museum. I took a lot of photos in the museum. In the garden of the museum, I saw kangaroos hopping around. For dinner, I met my uncle, who has lived in Auburn for 10 years. After dinner, we went to the musical, Wicked. I had a great time with him.
I hope this postcard finds you well. See you later back in school.

To : Ryan Park

From : Sarah Jung

✏️ **Writing Activities**

Use the action words : visited / walked / ate / met / saw / stayed / did / rode / toured / bought

_____
_____
_____
_____
_____
_____
_____
_____
_____
I hope this postcard finds you well. See you later back in school.

To : _____

From : _____

- ✂

Use the action words : visited / walked / ate / met / saw / stayed / did / rode / toured / bought

_____
_____
_____
_____
_____
_____
_____
_____
_____
I hope this postcard finds you well. See you later back in school.

To : _____

From : _____

74

3-2 Postcard from My Imaginary Vacation

Use the action words : visited / walked / ate / met / saw / stayed / did / rode / toured / bought

I hope this postcard finds you well. See you later back in school.

To : _____

From : _____

Use the action words : visited / walked / ate / met / saw / stayed / did / rode / toured / bought

I hope this postcard finds you well. See you later back in school.

To : _____

From : _____

✏️ **Writing Activities**

Use the action words : visited / walked / ate / met / saw / stayed / did / rode / toured / bought

_____
_____
_____
_____
_____
_____
_____
_____
_____
I hope this postcard finds you well. See you later back in school.

To : _____

From : _____

--✂

Use the action words : visited / walked / ate / met / saw / stayed / did / rode / toured / bought

_____
_____
_____
_____
_____
_____
_____
_____
_____
I hope this postcard finds you well. See you later back in school.

To : _____

From : _____

3-2 Postcard from My Imaginary Vacation

Use the action words : visited / walked / ate / met / saw / stayed / did / rode / toured / bought

I hope this postcard finds you well. See you later back in school.

To : _____

From : _____

Use the action words : visited / walked / ate / met / saw / stayed / did / rode / toured / bought

I hope this postcard finds you well. See you later back in school.

To : _____

From : _____

3-3

✏️ Writing Activities

Describe the Masterpiece Painting

Type
Solo work / Writing

Aim
To write a short paragraph about a painting

Level
Pre-intermediate ~ intermediate

Time
30 minutes

Language
Describing a painting

How to do the activity

1. 학생들에게 빔프로젝터를 통해서 Van Eyck의 "Giovanni Arnolfini and His Bride" 라는 그림을 보여 줍니다. 그림은 인터넷으로 쉽게 찾을 수 있습니다. 학생들에게는 화가와 작품의 이름을 미리 말해 주셔서는 안됩니다.

2. 학생들에게 그림을 볼 수 있는 시간을 10~20초 정도 줍니다. 그 후 그림과 관련된 다음과 같은 질문을 학생들에게 던집니다.

(Question 1) How many people are there in the room?
(Question 2) What color clothes is the man wearing? How does he look?
(Question 3) What are they doing in the room?
(Question 4) How does the woman feel? Why does she feel that way?

3. 학생들에게 79쪽의 worksheet을 나누어 줍니다. 교사와 방금 한 것처럼 학생들은 worksheet에 나와 있는 그림을 보고 주어진 질문에 답을 해야 합니다. 특히 자신의 상상력을 이용하여 대사를 만들어 내는 질문의 경우 좀 더 깊게 생각하도록 합니다.

4. 자신이 답한 문장을 이용하여 그 그림을 설명할 수 있는 짧은 글을 완성해 오는 과제를 제시합니다.

Teacher's Talk

1. Let's take a look at this painting. Now, I'm going to ask you some questions about it.

(Question 1) How many people are there in the room?
(Question 2) What color clothes is the man wearing? How does he look?
(Question 3) What are they doing in the room?
(Question 4) How does the woman feel? Why does she feel that way?

2. Now, I'm going to give you a worksheet showing two famous paintings as well as some questions about them. Answer the questions based on what you see and think about the paintings. I'll give you twenty minutes to complete it.

3. As a homework assignment, write a short paragraph describing each picture. Use the answers that you just wrote about the pictures for your writing.

Writing Activities

(Choice A : I take the seat)

① seat

② asleep

③ miss

④ late

Based on the pictures and the provided words, write a short paragraph.

I got on the bus to go to work. There was only one seat left on the bus. Because I was so tired, I ① _____ next to an old man. After a while, I ② _____ . So ③ _____ . I couldn't believe that I ④ _____ again.

Life Is Full of Choices

(Situation 1) To sit or not to sit. That is the question.

You're on the bus. There's only one seat left in the back of the bus. What would you do?

My Choice : _____

(Situation 2) Are you a sea person or mountain person?

You're planning a short trip with your boy/girlfriend. He/she wants to go to the beach, but you prefer to go camping on a quiet mountain. Where do you want to spend your summer break?

My Choice : _____

3-4 Life Is Full of Choices

✏️ **Writing Activities**

Type
Solo work / Writing

Aim
To write a short story in a guided activity

Level
Pre-intermediate

Time
50 minutes

Language
take the seat /
offer the seat /
fall asleep /
miss the bus /
have a conversation /
ask someone out

How to do the activity

1. 81쪽의 worksheet을 학생들에게 나누어 줍니다. worksheet에는 결정을 내려야 하는 상황 2가지가 제시되어 있습니다.

2. 첫 번째 상황은 버스에서의 자리 양보입니다. 학생들 각자는 자리를 양보할 것인가 혹은 그렇지 않을 것인가를 결정합니다. 자리 양보를 선택한 학생에게는 83쪽의 worksheet을 나누어 주고 주어진 그림과 힌트 단어를 이용하여 문장을 작성하도록 합니다. 문장 작성이 끝나면 그 문장들을 이용하여 하나의 단락을 만들도록 합니다. 자리를 양보하지 않는 것을 선택한 학생은 82쪽의 worksheet을 나누어 주고 동일하게 문장 및 단락을 만들도록 합니다. 교사와 함께 정답을 확인하도록 합니다.

3. 두 번째 상황은 여름철 휴가지를 결정하는 것입니다. 이 상황은 학생들에게 과제로 제시하도록 합니다. Writing 시 sample language를 제시했던 첫 번째 상황과는 달리 두 번째 상황은 바다나 산 중 하나를 선택하고 자신이 그 선택과 관련하여 그림을 그리고 문장을 만들어야 합니다. 그리고 그 문장을 연결하여 짧은 글을 하나 완성하도록 합니다.

Teacher's Talk

1. Life is full of choices. Today, I'm going to give you two situations where you need to make the best choice. The first situation is on a bus where there is only one empty seat. Are you going to take the seat? Or are you going to offer it to another person? Based on your decision, you will get a different worksheet. The worksheet shows what happens after you have made your decision. Using the provided pictures and words, write a short story.

2. Okay. It's time for you to make a decision. Who is going to take the seat? Raise your hand and I'll give you the worksheet. Who is going to offer the seat? Raise your hand, please. I'll give you a different worksheet. I'll give you five minutes to complete the paragraph.

3. (Five minutes later) Let's check the answers together.

4. The second decision that you need to make is about your vacation. Where do you want to go? Do you want to go to the beach or the mountain? Make a decision and then draw four pictures to describe what happens at the beach or in the mountain. You also need to write a short story to explain your pictures. If you cannot finish it today, it's going to be your homework assignment.

3-3 Describe the Masterpiece Painting

The Creation of Adam (Michelangelo, 1511)

Q1 : How many people are there in the picture besides the little angels?

Q2 : Is the man on the left wearing any clothes?

Q3 : What are the two people doing now?

Q4 : Why do you think they are doing it?

*Write a short paragraph about the painting. You can use the answers from the questions above.

School (Kim Hong Do, 18th century)

Q1 : Where are they?

Q2 : Who is the man behind the desk?

Q3 : What is the boy doing in front of the other boys?

Q4 : Why do you think he is crying?

Q5 : What do you think he is thinking now?

*Write a short paragraph about the painting. You can use the answers from the questions above.

3-4 Life Is Full of Choices

(Choice B : I offer the seat)

① offer

② conversation

③ ask

④ exchange

I got on the bus to go to work. There was only one seat left on the bus. Even though I was so tired, I didn't take the seat. Instead, ① _____. ② _____ with her. She said she's a huge fan of horror movies. I ③ _____. Just before I got off the bus at my stop, we ④ _____. My good intentions brought me good luck.

Writing Activities

(My Choice : I go to the beach / the mountain)

Based on the pictures, write a short story.

3-4 Life Is Full of Choices

Rate your friend's story.

Star Points	Your Comments

★★★ It's an excellent story.　　★★ It's ok.　　★ It's a horrible story.

Rate your friend's story.

Star Points	Your Comments

★★★ It's an excellent story.　　★★ It's ok.　　★ It's a horrible story.

Rate your friend's story.

Star Points	Your Comments

★★★ It's an excellent story.　　★★ It's ok.　　★ It's a horrible story.

✏️ **Writing Activities**

My Favorite TV Show

Type
Solo work / Writing

Aim
To write about their favorite TV shows

Level
Pre-intermediate

Time
30 minutes + Homework assignment

Language
My favorite TV show is ~ /
XXX stars in the show. /
I like it because ~
It is on channel 10

How to do the activity

1. 학생들에게 87쪽의 worksheet을 나누어 줍니다. 학생들은 자신이 가장 좋아하는 TV 프로그램을 하나 선정하여 worksheet 상단에 있는 질문에 대한 답을 간단하게 적도록 합니다.
2. 질문의 정답을 바탕으로 자신이 좋아하는 TV 프로그램에 대한 짧은 글을 쓰도록 합니다.

Teacher's Talk

1. Sarah, what's your favorite TV show? When can you watch it? Why do you like it? Okay, guess what we're going to talk about today. Yes, today's topic is all about TV shows.
2. Think about your favorite TV show. I'm sure you have a few shows that you enjoy watching, but choose only one.
3. Now, I'm going to give you a worksheet. First, answer the questions about your favorite show. You don't need to write full sentences in your answer. After that, use your answers to write a short paragraph about your favorite show.

Ryan's Tip

1. 수업시간에 작문을 모두 끝낼 수 없으면 과제로 제시하도록 합니다.
2. 한국 드라마 영어 수업에서 사용하기
① 학생들에게 가장 인기있는 드라마 한 장면을 보여 줍니다. 두명이 등장하는 드라마 장면이 좋습니다. 이렇게 하면 짝과 함께 활동을 진행할 수 있습니다.
② 학생들이 짝과 함께 그 장면의 대사를 영어로 옮기도록 합니다. 완벽한 영어가 아니어도 좋습니다. 의미만 전달될 수 있으면 됩니다.
③ 다시 드라마 장면을 보여 줍니다. 이 때 드라마 볼륨을 없애고 장면만 플레이되도록 합니다. 짝과 함께 학생들은 자신이 작성한 영어 대사를 캐릭터에 맞게 립싱크하면서 연습합니다. 마치 애니매이션에서 성우가 더빙을 하듯히 연습하면 됩니다.
④ 연습이 끝나면 학생들이 연습한 것을 발표하도록 합니다.
⑤ 영어 수준이 낮은 학생들은 교사와 함께 영어 대사를 작성하고 연습하도록 합니다.

My Favorite TV Show

1. Think about a TV show that you like to watch and fill in the blank.

      My Favorite TV Show : _____

2. Answer the following questions about your favorite show.

Questions	Answers
When is it on TV?	
Who stars in the TV show?	
What other TV shows did the main actors star in?	
Why do you like the show?	
Is there any similar show?	
Where is the show filmed (recorded)?	
What's your favorite episode?	
What do you think about the music (soundtrack)?	

3. Based on your answers above, write a short essay about your favorite TV show.

The TV show that I love to watch is _____

_____

_____

_____

_____

_____

_____

_____

_____

_____

_____

3-6 My Chart

Type of activity
Solo work / Writing

Aim of activity
To write sentences using student's own charts

Level
Pre-intermediate

Time
40 minutes

Language
comparison
(xxx times more than ~ /
taller than ~)

How to do the activity

1. 89쪽의 worksheet을 학생들 모두에게 나누어 줍니다.
2. 학생들은 3가지의 차트를 만들어야 합니다. 첫 번째 차트는 가족들의 키를 기록하는 차트입니다. 두 번째 차트는 일주일 동안 자신이 자주 먹는 음식을 기록하는 차트입니다. 마지막 차트는 친구들과 함께 만드는 것으로 자신이 가지고 있는 펜의 갯수를 기록하는 차트입니다.
3. 차트 제작이 끝나면 차트를 설명할 수 있는 문장을 만들어서 차트 옆에 기록하도록 합니다. 이 때 비교급을 이용하여 문장을 작성하도록 합니다.
4. 문장 작성이 끝나면 짝에게 자신의 차트를 설명하도록 합니다.

Teacher's Talk

1. I'm going to give you a handout that has three different charts. You need to complete each chart. The first chart is about the height of your family members. Make a bar chart showing how tall each of your family members is. The second chart is about your food intake for a week. Think about what you usually eat for a week and then make a pie chart. You need to work with your friends to make the last chart. Ask your friends how many pens they have right now and then make a bar chart. I'll give you 15 minutes to make the charts.
2. (After making the charts) Okay, it seems that you're finished with your chart-making. You'll see a blank next to each chart. On the blank, you need to write at least three sentences to explain the charts. For example, on the first chart, you can write who is taller than who or who is tallest (shortest) in your family. For the second chart, you can use "~ times more A than B." such as "I eat three times more rice than meat." I'll give you 15 minutes to complete your writing.
3. Compare what you wrote with your partner.

Ryan's Tip

1. 〈3〉번의 경우 차트를 만들기 위해서 다른 학생들과의 speaking 활동이 이루어져야 합니다. 학생들에게 "How many pens do you have?"라는 target expression을 사용하여 펜의 갯수를 조사 할 수 있도록 미리 주지시켜 주시기 바랍니다.

My Chart

Chart I : How Tall Are My Family Members?

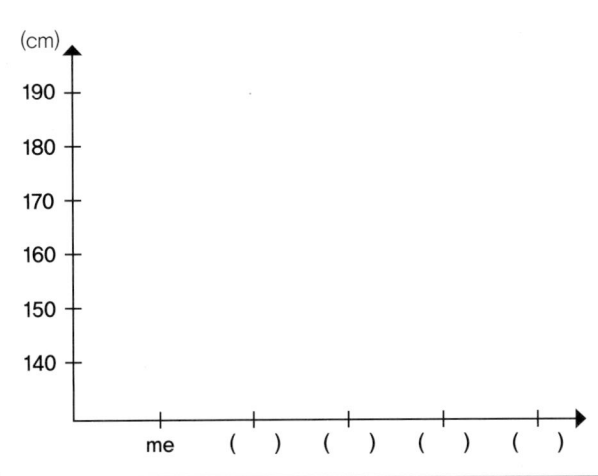

This chart shows how tall my family members are. First of all, the tallest person in my family is _____
_____
_____
_____
_____
_____
_____

Chart II : What Food Do I Eat For a Week? (%)

* rice
* vegetable
* bread
* snack
* meat
* others

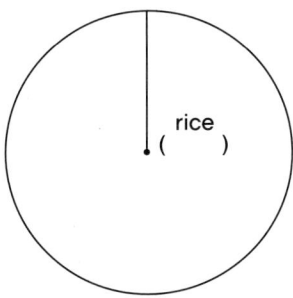

This chart explains my food intake for a week. As the chart shows, the food that I eat most is _____
_____
_____
_____
_____
_____
_____
_____

Chart III : How many pens do you have now?

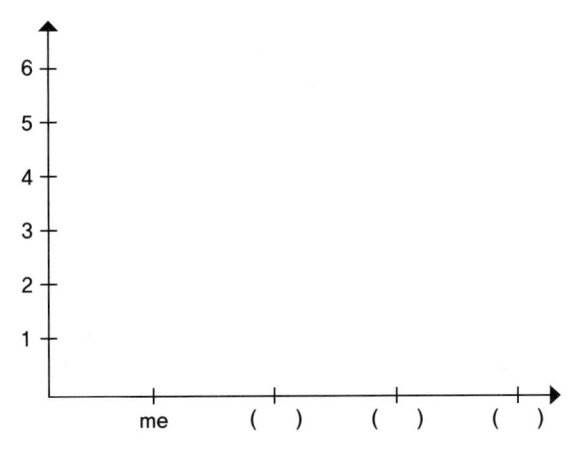

This chart shows how many pens my classmates have right now. According to the chart, _____ has the largest number of pens.
_____
_____
_____
_____
_____
_____

3-7 Describe This Job

Writing Activities

Type
Group work / Writing

Aim
To describe jobs

Level
Beginner ~
Pre-intermediate

Time
10 ~ 15 minutes

Language
1. Job titles
2. Expressions to describe jobs

How to do the activity

1. 4~5명이 한 조가 되도록 합니다.
2. 교사가 91쪽의 직업과 연관된 표현들을 불러줍니다. 학생들은 잘 듣고 어떤 직업인지 맞추어야 합니다.
3. 정답을 가장 많이 맞춘 팀이 승리합니다.
4. 직업을 맞추는 게임이 끝난 뒤 학생들 모두에게 교사가 사용하였던 91쪽의 worksheet을 나누어 줍니다.
5. 학생들은 worksheet에 있는 단어를 이용하여 91쪽의 worksheet에 그 직업을 소개하는 간단한 글을 작성하도록 합니다.

Teacher's Talk

1. Let's make groups of four students.
2. Now, I'm going to tell you some phrases related to a job. As a group, listen carefully to the phrases and try to guess what kind of job I'm talking about. If you think you know the answer, just call out your group name.
3. (After the game is over) I'm going to give you the worksheet that I used for this game. First, choose a job that you're most interested in. Next, using the words from the worksheet, you need to write a short paragraph introducing the job. Let's take a look at the worksheet together. Do you have any words that you are not familiar with?

Ryan's Tip

1. 게임 도중 학생들이 모르는 단어가 나와도 게임을 중단하지 않는 것이 좋습니다. 나중에 worksheet을 나누어 주고 게임에서 몰랐던 표현을 익히는 시간을 가질 것이기 때문입니다.
2. 글을 완성한 뒤 자신은 어떤 직업을 가지고 싶은지에 대해서 간단하게 질문하는 것도 좋습니다.
3. 이 활동이 끝나고 난 뒤 92쪽에 있는 resume 쓰는 활동을 연결시켜 주면 자신의 미래 직업과 관련된 수업을 구상할 수 있습니다.

Describe This Job

Actor	Cook	Doctor
1. live many different lives 2. famous 3. perform in the theater 4. have agents or managers	1. work with fire 2. wash hands before work 3. cut, saute, peel, chop 4. enjoy eating food	1. study all the time 2. work long hours 3. should like to help people 4. make sick people healthier

Firefighter	Architect	Lawyer
1. dangerous work 2. brave 3. wear heavy clothes and masks 4. save people in burning buildings	1. design 2. create drawings for clients 3. good at math, physics 4. make houses, schools or huge buildings	1. take people's side 2. write legal documents 3. make arguments 4. should win in court

Musician (singer)	Police officer	Reporter
1. must have talent 2. play with instruments 3. compose, sing or play music 4. perform in concerts	1. wear uniforms 2. healthy and strong 3. prevent crimes 4. enforce laws	1. must meet deadlines 2. talk to a lot of people 3. study journalism 4. write news stories for TV or newspapers

Writer	Secretary	Teacher
1. make a story 2. should read a lot 3. do research before work 4. write novels, columns or articles	1. type very fast 2. work in office 3. put files in order 4. help their boss	1. explain information or theories 2. grade papers 3. study all the time 4. take care of students

Choose a job that you're interested in and write a short paragraph about the job. You can use the phrases above.

_____

_____

_____

_____

_____

_____

3-8 Create Your Future Resume

✏️ **Writing Activities**

Type
Solo work / Writing

Aim
To write a resume

Level
Pre-intermediate ~ Intermediate

Time
40 minutes +
Homework assignment

Language
Vocabulary related to resume writing

How to do the activity

1. 학생들에게 93쪽의 resume sample을 나누어 줍니다.

2. 학생들에게 resume sample을 2분 동안 읽도록 한 뒤 다음에 질문에 답하도록 합니다.

(**Question 1**) What university did James graduate?
(**Question 2**) What did he study at Boston College? When did he go to the college?
(**Question 3**) What did he do in 2003?
(**Question 4**) What did he achieve in 2004?
(**Question 5**) Did he write a book? When / what did he write?
(**Question 6**) What language is he able to speak?

3. 학생들이 자신의 미래 이력서를 작성하도록 합니다. 지원하는 직업, 학력, 경력, 기술 등의 요소들을 상상하여 미래 이력서를 작성하도록 합니다. 이력서 형태는 93쪽에 제시된 James의 sample을 따르도록 합니다.

4. 완성된 이력서는 게시판에 붙여 놓습니다.

Teacher's Talk

1. I'm going to give you Mr. James Donaldson's resume. Read it and answer the questions.

2. (After asking questions about the resume) Now, I want you to write your own future resume. First, think about what kind of job you want to apply for. Based on that job, create your educational background, career experiences, achievements, and skills. Use your imagination.

3. This is a homework assignment. Type your resume on the computer at home.

Ryan's Tip

1. 이력서 양식은 졸업후에도 다시 사용할 수 있으므로 수업시간에 작성한 이력서를 컴퓨터로 다시 옮겨 작성한 후 파일로 보관해 놓도록 하는 것이 좋습니다.

2. 영어 수준이 낮은 경우 샘플을 충분히 익힌 후 자신의 이력서를 작성하도록 합니다.

3. 제가 대학교 4학년 영어회화 시간에 했던 활동을 응용해 보았습니다.

James Donaldson

803 Ho 101 Dong, Samku APT
Hankil dong, Kangdong gu, Seoul, Korea
(123) 456-7890
abcdeg @ yahee.com

Objective
Seeking a position as an elementary education teacher in Greenland School District

Education
1992	High School Diploma, Kimberly High School, California
1996	B.A., Early Childhood Education, Harvard University
2009	M.A., Elementary Education, Boston College

Experience
1996 – 1998	Receptionist / Academic Counselor, EBC Academy
1998 – 1999	Full-time Instructor of English, Youth Challenge Academy
2000 – 2003	Assistant Manager, Youth Challenge Academy
2004 – 2005	Part-time Instructor of Math & Science, Boston Institute of Education
2005 – 2009	Private Tutor for five high school students

Achievement / Certificate
2000	Interpreter Certificate of Korean – English
2002	First Grade of Computer Technician Certificate
2004	1ST place in National English Essay Contest
2009	Book Publication (Title: How to teach kindergarten)

Skill
Fluent in English, Spanish, and Korean
Proficient in computer (MS Office, Apple Software)
Proficient in teenager counseling

3-9 Plan Your Date

✎ Writing Activities

Type
Solo work / Writing

Aim
To plan an imaginary date

Level
Intermediate

Time
50 minutes

Language
I'm going to / I will / I want to

How to do the activity

1. 95~96쪽의 worksheet을 양면복사하여 각 학생들에게 나누어 줍니다. 각 학생들은 이번 주말에 있을 남자 / 여자 친구와의 데이트를 가상으로 계획해야 합니다. 그들에게 주어진 데이트 시간은 하루이며, 100,000원의 용돈을 지급 받습니다.

2. 95~96쪽의 plan your date에 나와 있는 음식과 교통편, 할 일, 갈 곳 등을 적절하게 선택하도록 합니다. 선택한 아이템의 가격을 97쪽의 표에 기록하여 최종 지출이 100,000원이 넘지 않도록 합니다.

3. 자신이 선택한 데이트 아이템들을 이용하여 아래의 빈 칸에 하나의 짧은 글을 작성합니다. 미래에 할 일이므로 미래 시제를 사용하도록 합니다.

4. 학생들의 작문이 끝나면 모든 학생들의 handout을 걷습니다.

5. 학생들에게 다른 학생의 date plan을 나누어 줍니다. 학생들은 date plan을 읽은 뒤 별표로 점수를 주도록 합니다. 그리고 그 데이트에 대한 자신들의 의견을 쓸 수 있도록 합니다. 표에서 주어진 것과 같이 별점을 줄 수도 있습니다.

6. 2분 정도가 지나면 다시 학생들의 date plan을 걷습니다. 그리고 또 다른 학생들의 date plan을 주고 학생들이 평가하도록 합니다. 이 활동을 3회 정도 합니다.

7. 9개의 별표를 받은 학생이 그 반에서 가장 romantic한 학생으로 선발됩니다.

Teacher's Talk

1. You're going on your very first date with your boy/girlfriend this weekend. Your mom gave you 100,000 won for the special day. Now, let's plan the perfect date.

2. I'm going to give you this Plan Your Date worksheet where you'll see what you can do, eat, ride, and buy on your date. Decide what you want to do by circling the pictures on the chart. Make sure you write down the price of each item on the chart. You MUST NOT spend more than 100,000 won.

3. Now, it's time to write about your plan. Below the price chart, write a short paragraph using the items you circled. Make sure to plan your date in detail.

4. (After collecting students' writing) Now, I'm going to give you someone else's date plan. You need to read it and then give star points. If you think the date plan is really good, give 3 stars. If you think it's ok, give 2 stars. If it is not that great, give just one star. After giving star points, you need to make some comments.

Ryan's Tip

1. 한국에는 유난히 사랑을 고백할 수 있는 날들이 많이 있죠? 발렌타인데이, 화이트데이, 빼빼로데이 등에 이 활동을 하면 학생들에게 큰 호응이 있습니다.

2. 학생들이 데이트를 계획하고 작문하는데 시간이 많이 걸리면 과제로 제시하고 다음 차시에서 평가를 할 수 있도록 합니다.

Plan Your Date

You're going on a date with your boy / girlfriend this weekend. Plan your date with 100,000 won. Circle the pictures of what you want to do and then write the price on the chart. The price of the items is for two people.

Transportation	Walk	City Bus	Subway	Bike	Taxi	Rental Car
Cost (won)	Free	3,000	3,000	3,000	20,000	40,000

Food 1	Hamburger	Street food	Chinese	Japanese	Italian	Korean
Cost (won)	7,000	5,000	10,000	15,000	20,000	15,000

Food 2	Hotel Restaurant	Lunch Box	Hot Dog	Ice Cream	Coffee	Coke
Cost (won)	60,000	5,000	5,000	10,000	10,000	5,000

✏️ **Writing Activities**

	Movie	Musical	Concert	Opera	Amusement Park	Zoo
Entertainment 1						
Cost (won)	30,000	60,000	50,000	75,000	45,000	40,000

	3D Movie	Museum	Art Gallery	Window Shopping	Biking	Riding Ferry
Entertainment 2						
Cost (won)	40,000	20,000	30,000	Free	15,000	35,000

	Hiking	PC Bang	Singing Room	JimJil Bang	Bookstore	Park
Entertainment 3						
Cost (won)	15,000	25,000	40,000	30,000	Free	Free

	Flower	Music CD	Book	Balloon	Ring	Doll
Present						
Cost (won)	15,000	20,000	20,000	10,000	50,000	30,000

3-9 Plan Your Date

How much do you spend?

Items (Things to do)	Cost
Total	

What do you do on your date?

Tomorrow, I'm going to have a date with _____ (person's name).

I'm so excited to go out with him / her. First, we're going to _____

_____

_____

_____

_____

_____

_____

_____

Rate your friend's date.

Star Points	Your Comments

★★★ It's my dream date.   ★★ It's ok.   ★ It's a horrible date.

3-10 Publish the School Newspaper

Type
Group work / Writing

Aim
To make a school newspaper

Level
Intermediate

Time
50 minutes (1st lesson) +
50 minutes (2nd lesson)

Language
Writing newspaper articles

✏️ **Writing Activities**

How to do the activity

〔 Lesson 1 〕

1. 4명이 한 모둠이 되도록 합니다. 모든 학생들은 99쪽의 newspaper brainstorming worksheet을 받습니다. 학생들이 제작할 영어 신문은 4개의 섹션으로 나누어 져 있습니다. 학생들은 신문의 이름을 정하고 각 섹션에 맞게 어떤 소재에 대해 기사를 쓸 지 정해야 합니다. 그리고 모둠 중에서 누가 취재를 하고 기사를 쓸지를 결정해야 합니다. 4명이 한 모둠이므로 각 학생이 한 섹션씩 분담해서 맡습니다.

2. worksheet에 나와 있는 질문에 답하면서 자신이 쓸 기사에 대한 brainstorming을 시작합니다. 기사를 실제로 쓰는 것은 수업 중에 하는 것이 아니라 과제로 제시하도록 합니다. 기사의 길이는 학생의 수준에 따라 다르지만 보통 A4 사이즈 반 쪽 정도가 적당합니다. 사진 혹은 이미지가 들어갈 공간을 생각하면 그 정도가 좋습니다.

3. 학생들은 다음시간까지 자신이 할당받은 기사를 작성해야 합니다.

〔 Lesson 2 〕

1. 지난 시간과 동일한 모둠으로 앉습니다.

2. 학생들은 자신이 작성해 온 영어 기사를 같은 모둠의 학생들에게 보여 줍니다. 다른 학생들의 신문 기사를 읽으면서 학생들은 자신의 의견을 이야기 합니다. 만일 과제로 신문 기사를 써 오지 않은 학생이 있다면 이번 시간에 신문 기사를 완성할 수 있도록 합니다.

3. 신문 기사에 대한 review가 끝나면 신문 완성에 대한 차후의 계획을 상의합니다. 어디서, 언제 만나서 신문 편집과 디자인을 완성할지 결정하도록 합니다.

4. 다음 시간까지 신문을 완성해서 제출하도록 합니다. 제출된 신문은 학교 게시판에 게시하도록 합니다.

Teacher's Talk

1. During the next two lessons, we're going to publish a school newspaper. Since it's a group project, I want you to make a group of four students.

2. Now, I'm going to give you a worksheet to help you brainstorm the articles you want to write. Your newspaper should have at least four different sections. Since you have four group members, each member should choose a section to write an article about.

3. Now, within your group, discuss what topics you're going to write about for each section. Do NOT decide the topics by yourself. This is not a personal newspaper. After you choose your topics, you need to individually answer the questions for your section of the newspaper. By answering the questions, you'll start to get a clear picture of your article.

4. Before the end of class, you should decide on the name of your newspaper and write the title on the worksheet. As homework, you should complete writing the article that you're assigned today. In addition, think about the photos and visual images related to your article.

5. (In the next lesson) Did you finish your article? Show your article to your group members. After reading your group members' article, you need to give some feedback. If they need to make some changes, you need to tell them today. If you didn't complete your article, you have to finish it now.

6. If you think your articles are good enough to be published in the paper, then you need to talk about when and where to meet to design or edit your newspaper. You should finish making your newspaper this week so that you can bring the final newspaper to the next lesson. Once again, it's a group project, which means everyone in your group should work together to make a good newspaper.

3-10 Publish the School Newspaper

Title of the newspaper :

Group members :

The Biggest School Event :

* Brainstorm the article by answering the questions below.

1. What happened?
2. Who was there?
3. Why did it happen?
4. When did it happen?
5. Where did it happen?
6. Additional information :

* Who is writing the article?

Interview :

* Make a plan for the interview.

1. Who are you going to interview?
2. Who is interviewing the person?
3. When / Where are you going to interview?
4. What questions are we going to ask?

* Who is writing the article?

Next Meeting : (when)

(where)

The Biggest Class Event :

* Brainstorm the article by answering the questions below.

1. What happened?
2. Who was there?
3. Why did it happen?
4. When did it happen?
5. Where did it happen?
6. Additional information :

* Who is writing the article?

* You can do anything that you want with this section. Cartoon, movie review, book review, weather, sports, entertainment, Photo, editorial... You name it. Everything is possible.

* Topic :

* Make a plan for this section :

1. If necessary, who is drawing pictures?
2. What sport / movie / book are you going to deal with?
3. Additional Information:

* Who will take this section?

UNIT 4

Grammar
Activities

UNIT 4 Grammar Activities

4-1	Create a Super Hero (p.70 ~ p.71)
Type	Solo work
Aim	To practice the subjunctive mood through a controlled activity
Level	Pre-intermediate
Time	20 minutes

4-2	English Class Rules (p.72 ~ p.77)
Type	Group work
Aim	To set up class rules
Level	All level
Time	15 ~ 20 minutes

4-3	Draw Public Manners (p.78 ~ p.79)
Type	Group work
Aim	To practice imperative through art activity
Level	Beginner ~ pre-intermediate
Time	25 minutes

4-4	Subway Ride (p.80 ~ p.85)
Type	Solo work
Aim	To practice three tenses (past, present perfect, past perfect)
Level	All level
Time	10 minutes

4-5	Who Is This Person? (p.86 ~ p.87)
Type	Pair work
Aim	To practice proper use of pronouns
Level	Beginner
Time	15 minutes

4-6	Wonderful Buildings (p.88 ~ p.89)
Type	Pair work
Aim	To practice passive form with information gap activity
Level	Beginner
Time	10 minutes

4-7	World History Map (p.90 ~ p.91)
Type	Pair work
Aim	To practice past tense using world's history
Level	Beginner ~ pre-intermediate
Time	20 minutes

4-8	Grammar Auction (p.92 ~ p.93)
Type	Group work
Aim	To review previous grammar lesson
Level	All level
Time	10 ~ 15 minutes

4-9	What Will Happen Next (p.94 ~ p.97)
Type	Pair work
Aim	To practice future tense
Level	Beginner
Time	10 ~ 15 minutes

4-10	Grammar Battleship (p.98 ~ p.99)
Type	Group work
Aim	To review previous grammar lesson
Level	All level
Time	10 ~ 15 minutes

Grammar Activities

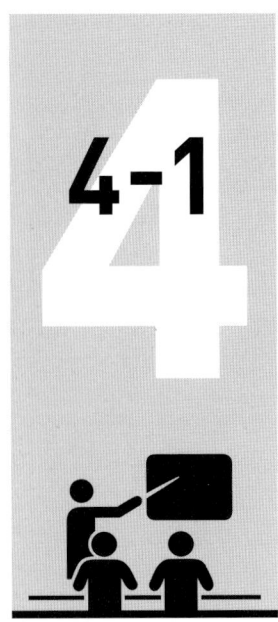

4-1 Create a Super Hero

How to do the activity

1. 가정법 과거를 충분히 학습한 뒤 이 활동을 하도록 합니다.
2. 학생들에게 103쪽의 worksheet을 나누어 줍니다. worksheet에는 20가지의 super powers가 나열되어 있습니다. 자신이 super hero가 될 것을 가정하고 최강의 super hero가 되기 위해 자신이 필요한 super powers를 5가지만 고르도록 합니다.
3. 자신이 고른 super powers 5가지를 가지고 샘플 문장과 같이 가정법 과거 형태를 사용하여 문장을 만들도록 합니다. 문장을 완성한 뒤 자신의 캐릭터의 이름을 짓고, 그 캐릭터와 어울리는 의상을 그려 주도록 합니다.
4. 자신의 super hero를 짝에게 보여 준 뒤 가장 재미있는 super powers 문장을 고르도록 합니다. 학생들의 worksheet을 모두 걷어 게시판에 게시합니다.

Teacher's Talk

1. Today, you're going to be a super hero who saves the world from evil. On the worksheet, you'll see twenty super powers. Choose five super powers from the worksheet and write what you would do if you had those super powers. You should use the sentence pattern provided on the worksheet. In addition, you need to draw a picture of yourself wearing a super hero costume such as boots, a cape, weapons, etc. I'll give you 10 minutes to complete this task.
2. (10 minutes later) Exchange your worksheet with a partner. Read your partner's sentences and then choose the sentence with the most brilliant idea.

Ryan's Tip

1. 문법을 본격적으로 설명하기 전에 먼저 그림을 이용하여 상황을 제시해 보세요. 그림은 간단하고 명확하게 설명을 할 수 있고, 학생들의 관심을 집중시킬 수 있다는 점에서 아주 효과적인 상황 제시 방법입니다. 활동에서 사용되는 가정법을 설명하는 수업의 경우에는 다음과 같은 그림을 먼저 제시할 수 있습니다.

Type
Solo work / Grammar

Aim
To practice the subjunctive mood through a controlled activity

Level
Pre-intermediate

Time
20 minutes

Language
If I had ~, I would ~

그리고 난 후 그림과 관련된 다음과 같은 질문을 던집니다.
Teacher : Who is this?
Students : 학생들 여러 이름을 부른다.
Teacher : Ok. This is Jae-won.
Look at the picture. Is he happy now?
Students : No.
Teacher : Why isn't he happy?
Students : No money. Beggar...
Teacher : What is he thinking now?
Students : Money.... buy a car.
Teacher : Can you make it in a sentence?

이 후에 가정법에 대해서 설명을 해 주시면 됩니다.

4-1 Create a Super Hero

Create a Super Hero

Choose five super powers that you wish to have as a super hero.

( ) live without eating any food
( ) fly without flapping wings
( ) turn everything into ice
( ) read people's mind
( ) absorb energy from living creatures
( ) finish reading a book in a minute
( ) move at lightning speed
( ) operate any kind of machine / car
( ) hear a pin drop within 50 miles
( ) heal the injured in a second

( ) control weather
( ) teleport
( ) predict the future
( ) communicate with animals
( ) be invisible
( ) speak 20 foreign languages
( ) stretch your body into any form
( ) change into any human
( ) see ghosts
( ) burn everything into flames

What would you do if you had those super powers?

Draw Your Super Hero.
(Hero's Name: _____)

(sample) If I had the super power to <u>control weather</u>, I would <u>keep the weather in my neighborhood always sunny with no rain.</u>

1. If I had the super power to _____
I would _____

2. If I had the super power to _____
I would _____

3. If I _____
I would _____

4. If I _____
I would _____

5. If I _____
I would _____

📝 **Grammar Activities**

4-2 English Class Rules

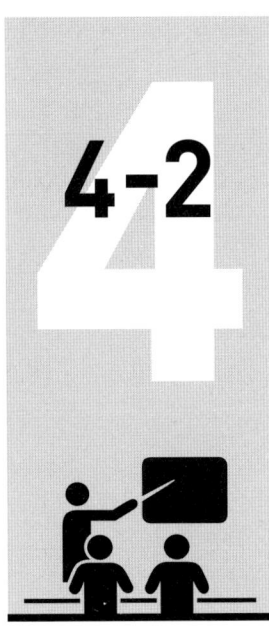

Type
Group work / Grammar + Writing + Speaking

Aim
To set up class rules

Level
All level

Time
15 ~ 20 minutes

Language
Imperative
(Do ~ / Don't ~)

How to do the activity

1. 4명이 한 조가 되도록 합니다.
2. 105쪽에 있는 English Class Rules worksheet을 각 조에 나누어 줍니다. 학생들이 상의하여 영어 시간에 지켜야 할 규칙을 Do~ 와 Don't ~로 나누어 적도록 합니다.
3. 첫 번째 조의 학생들부터 규칙을 하나씩 읽도록 합니다. 만일 다른 조에 비슷한 규칙이 있으면 그 규칙에 동그라미를 치도록 합니다. 첫 번째 조의 발표가 끝나면 두 번째 조가 발표를 하는데 이미 동그라미 친 것은 읽지 않고 아직 발표가 안 된 규칙을 읽도록 합니다. 이렇게 해야지 시간이 절약되고 또한 모든 조가 발표를 할 수 있습니다. 마지막 조까지 읽지 않은 규칙을 발표시킵니다.
4. 가장 동그라미가 많이 나왔던 규칙을 우리 반의 규칙으로 제정합니다.

Teacher's Talk

1. Today, you're going to make some class rules. First, I want you to make groups of four students. I'm going to give you a worksheet. Within your group, write five do's and don'ts that students should keep in this class. For example, you can write down, "Don't sleep in class" or "Bring your book." I'll give you five minutes to complete your class rules.
2. (5 minutes later) Okay. Group 1. Would you read the rules that you made? Everyone, if group 1 tells similar rules that your group made, you need to circle them on your worksheet. Group 1, read your rules, please. Thank you, group 1. Now, let's move on to Group 2. Group 2, don't read the rules that group 1 already said. Read the new rules that they didn't say yet.

Ryan's Tip

1. 명령문을 이용한 활동입니다. 하반의 경우 명령문이 무엇인지 잠시 설명해 주고 활동을 하는 것이 좋습니다.
2. 우리 반의 규칙을 만들고 난 뒤 다음 시간에 규칙을 정리해서 아이들에게 보여 주세요. 그리고 모든 학생들의 서명을 받은 뒤 교실에 붙여 둡니다. 학생들이 규칙을 어길 때마다 서명이 적힌 규정을 한번씩 보여 주는 것도 좋겠죠? 캐나다 초등학교의 한 교실에서 사용하였던 것을 적용해 보았습니다.

English Class Rules

Group members : _____ _____ _____ _____

Do This!

1. _____
2. _____
3. _____
4. _____
5. _____

Don't Do This!

1. _____
2. _____
3. _____
4. _____
5. _____

4-3 Draw Public Manners

📝 **Grammar Activities**

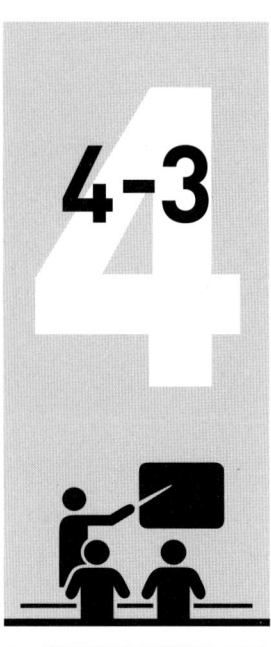

Type
Group work / Grammar + Speaking

Aim
To practice imperative through art activity

Level
Beginner ~ Pre-intermediate

Time
25 minutes

Language
Imperative
(Do ~ / Don't ~)

How to do the activity

1. 107~108쪽에 있는 각 문장의 단어를 잘라서 각각 조그만 봉투에 집어 넣습니다.
2. 4명이 한 모둠을 만들도록 합니다. 각 모둠에게 단어가 들어 있는 봉투 하나씩을 나누어 줍니다.
3. "Ready. Get Set. Go!"의 신호와 함께 각 모둠의 학생들은 봉투 속에 있는 단어들을 배열하여 명령문 문장을 만들도록 합니다.
4. 배열한 명령문의 내용에 맞게 모둠의 모든 학생들이 협동하여 109쪽의 하나의 단체 그림을 그리도록 합니다. 내용을 가장 효과적으로 전달할 수 있도록 그림을 크고 간결하게 그리도록 지시합니다. 문장을 배열하고 그림을 그리는 제한시간은 7분입니다. 절대 7분을 벗어날 수 없습니다.
5. 7분 뒤 각 분단의 그림을 수합합니다. 교사가 학생들의 그림을 보여 주면 그 그림을 그린 팀을 제외한 나머지 팀이 어떤 명령문인지 맞춥니다. 가장 많이 맞추는 팀이 승리 팀이 됩니다.

Teacher's Talk

1. Let's make a group of four students. I'm going to give an envelope to each group. Each envelope has words in it. Your group needs to put the words in order to make a proper sentence.
2. When you're finished, draw a big picture based on the sentence. You must draw together as a team...NOT ALONE!!
3. Time is very important today. You'll have only 7 minutes to complete your sentence and picture.
4. (7 minutes later) Time's up! Please give me your pictures. Now, I'm going to show you the pictures, and you need to tell me the sentence of each group's drawing.

Ryan's Tip

1. 활동이 끝난 다음 그림들을 수합하여 교실의 게시판 등에 "Public Manners"라는 제목으로 전시를 하는 것도 좋습니다.
2. 각 모둠에서 문장을 배열하는 동안에는 목소리를 낮추어 다른 모둠의 학생들이 엿듣지 않도록 해야 합니다.
3. 그림을 한 학생이 그리지 않도록 합니다. 이런 미술을 이용하는 활동에서 특히 한 학생이 지배적으로 활동을 이끌어 나가는 경향이 있으므로 세심한 모니터링이 필요합니다.

4-3 Draw Public Manners

movie theater	in the	cell phone	your	turn off
street	in the	a ball game	play	don't
full	your mouth	with	speak	don't
street	the	on	spit	don't
bus	on the	loudly	talk	don't

Grammar Activities

meetings	escalator	the street	subway	subway
for your	on the	crossing	on the	on the
late	run	before	or drink	to the elderly
be	not	both ways	eat	your seat
don't	do	look	don't	offer

108

4-3 Draw Public Manners

Public Manner :

4-4 Subway Ride

Grammar Activities

Type
Solo work / Grammar

Aim
To practice three tenses (past, present perfect, past perfect)

Level
All level

Time
10 minutes

Language
Past / present perfect / past perfect

How to do the activity

1. 학생들에게 111쪽의 worksheet을 나누어 줍니다.
2. 학생들에게 1번부터 7번까지의 시제와 관련된 문제를 풀도록 합니다. worksheet에 나와 있는 지시사항대로 과거시제를 선택하면 지하철이 한 정거장 앞으로 이동합니다. 현재완료시제를 선택하면 지하철이 두 정거장 앞으로 이동하며, 과거완료시제를 선택하면 세 정거장 이동합니다.
3. 문제를 다 풀고 난 뒤 어떤 역에 지하철이 도착했는지 적도록 합니다.
4. 교사와 함께 각 문제에 대한 정답을 알아 보도록 합니다.

Teacher's Talk

1. Since we learned about present perfect and past perfect tenses during our last class, I want to do an activity using the tenses. I'm going to give you a worksheet that has seven questions about the tenses. You need to choose the correct tense for each question. If you choose the past tense, the subway moves one stop forward. If you choose the present perfect (have + p.p), the subway moves two stops forward. If you choose the past perfect (had + p.p), the subway moves three stops forward.
2. After solving all the questions, you'll see the final stop of your subway.

Ryan's Tip

1. 여기서는 시제 문제를 사용하였으나 다른 문법 사항을 가르칠 때 문제만 다르게 제시하고 worksheet에 있는 지하철 지도만 오려서 사용하면 이 활동을 계속 재활용할 수 있습니다.
2. 간단한 문법 문제풀이도 이렇게 약간의 재미를 붙여주면 학생들이 스스로 학습하는데 동기를 제공해 줄 수 있습니다. 어떻게 보면 문법 문제 풀이에 목적을 부여해 주는 것이라고 할 수 있겠죠.

문법문제 정답

1. had been **2.** slept **3.** had given **4.** had locked **5.** moved **6.** had left
7. has been

《출처 : 영문법 훈련노트 1 (박용호, 길벗이지톡)》

Subway Ride

1. You should choose the correct tense for each sentence.
   - *If you choose **the past tense**, the subway moves **one stop** forward.*
   - *If you choose the present perfect (**have + p.p**), the subway moves **two stops** forward.*
   - *If you choose the past perfect (**had + p.p**), the subway moves **three stops** forward.*

2. After solving all the questions, you'll see the final stop of your subway.

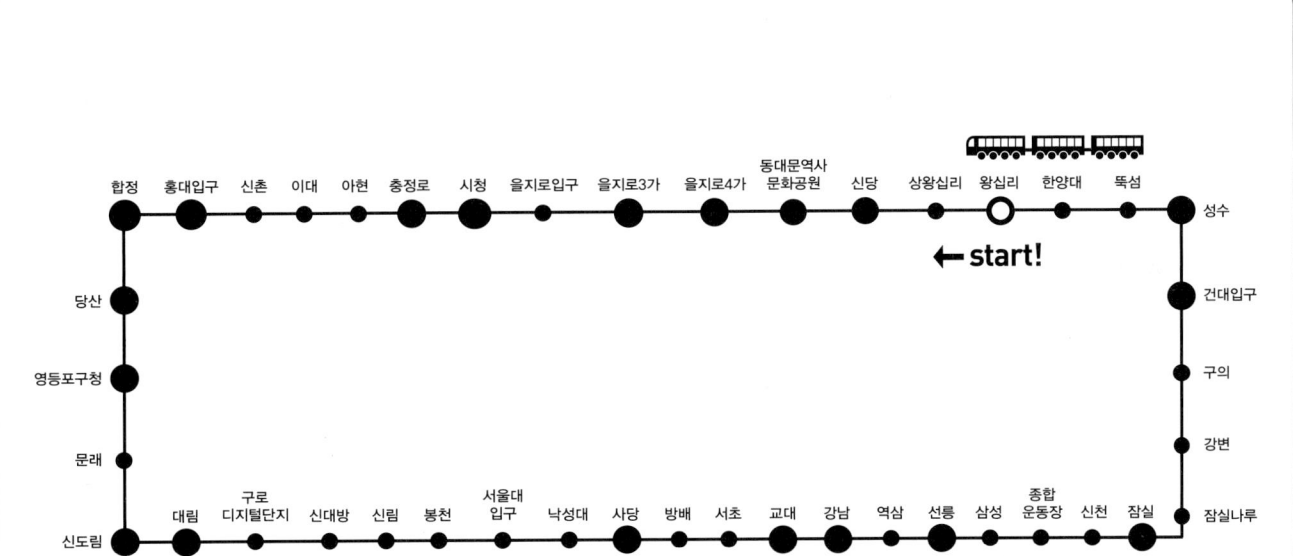

Choose the right words.

1. Before he got married to the rich girl, he (was / had been / have been) unemployed.
2. I (slept / have slept) in the living room last night.
3. She was very sad to hear that her father (has given / had given) away her pony to charity.
4. I thought that I (had locked / has locked) the door, but I didn't.
5. She (moved / has moved) to the new town 5 years ago.
6. When I came to the party, most of them (have left / had left) already.
7. James (has been / was) the team leader since 2005.

The final stop of your subway : _____

4-5 Who Is This Person?

📝 **Grammar Activities**

Type
Pair work / Grammar

Aim
To practice proper use of pronouns

Level
Beginner

Time
15 minutes

Language
Pronouns

How to do the activity

1. he, her, they, their 등 대명사의 용법을 배우고 난 뒤 사용하는 활동입니다.
2. 학생들에게 113쪽의 worksheet 윗 쪽을 잘라 나누어 줍니다. 제시된 인물의 정보를 이용하여 문장의 빈칸을 채우도록 지시합니다. 또한 괄호에는 문장에 적절한 인칭대명사를 고르도록 합니다.
3. 교사와 함께 정답을 맞추어 봅니다.
4. 학생들을 A 와 B로 나눕니다. A 학생은 113쪽 worksheet의 A 부분을, B 학생은 113쪽 worksheet의 B 부분을 받습니다. 그 후 앞에서 한 것과 동일하게 제시된 인물의 정보를 이용하여 문장의 빈칸에 채우도록 합니다. 물론 적절한 대명사도 골라야 합니다. 절대로 A 학생과 B 학생이 자신의 worksheet을 보여 주어서는 안됩니다.
5. 빈 칸 작성이 끝났으면 자신이 작성한 문장을 파트너에게 읽어 줍니다. 파트너는 문장을 듣고 누구를 설명하는 것인지 맞추도록 합니다.

Teacher's Talk

1. I'm going to give you a worksheet. You need to fill in the blanks using the provided information and circle the proper pronoun for each sentence. When you're done, guess who the short story is talking about. I'll give you two minutes.
2. (Two minutes later) Okay, let's check the answers together. Heeju, would you read the sentences?
3. Now, let's move on to the next activity. First, you need to choose a partner and then decide who's going to be Student A and who's going to be Student B. Student A will get worksheet A and student B will get worksheet B. You MUST NOT show your worksheet to your partner.
4. Just as you did in the previous activity, you should fill in the blanks and circle the proper pronoun for each sentence. Once you're finished, read your sentences to your partner, and he/she should guess who the short story is talking about.
5. Once again. You MUST NOT show your worksheet to your partner.

〈출처: 영문법 훈련노트 1 (박용호, 길벗이지톡)〉

4-5 Who Is This Person?

> **?**
>
> * Birth : England, 1961
> * Ex-husband : Prince Charles
> * Sons : Prince William / Prince Harry
> * Job : Princess of Wales
> * Death : car accident
>
> *Birth* 탄생 / *princess* 공주

(Her / She) was born in _____ in 1961. (Her / She) was married to _____. She wore a beautiful gown at (her / she) wedding. (Her / She) gave birth to Prince _____ , and two years later (her / she) second son, Prince _____ was born. As Princess of _____ , (her / she) did a lot of charity work such as helping children with AIDS. (Her / She) died in a _____ accident with (her / she) boyfriend. Many people were sad at (her / she) funeral. Who is (her / she)?

Give birth to 낳다 / *charity* 자선 / *funeral* 장례식

-- ✂

Worksheet A
Choose the proper pronouns. Also, fill in the blanks with the provided information.

> **?**
>
> * Birth : Macedonia, 1910
> * Job : nun at the age of 18
> * Charity work : worked as a teacher in India / looked after the poor
> * Award : The Nobel Peace Prize

(Her / She) was born in _____ in 1910. (Her / She) became a nun at the age of 18. In (her / she) early years, she worked as a _____ in India. After seeing people in need in India, (her / she) decided to look after _____ for the rest of (her / she) life. (Her / She) won the _____ Prize in 1979. Until (her / she) last illness, (her / she) served the people who needed (her / she) help. Who is (her / she)?

-- ✂

Worksheet B
Choose the proper pronouns. Also, fill in the blanks with the provided information.

> **?**
>
> * Birth : America, 1847
> * Education : quit school / study at home
> * Achievement : invented many devices
> * Death : diabetes
>
> *invent* 발명하다 / *diabetes* 당뇨병

(His / He) was born in _____ in 1847. (Him / He) quit school when he was young. So, (he / his) mother taught (he / him) at _____. (He / Him) invented many _____ such as a motion picture camera and a light bulb. (He / him) died of complications of _____ in 1931 in (he / his) home. Without (his / him) inventions, we may still live in the darkness. Who is (him / he)?

motion picture 영화 / *light bulb* 전구 / *complications* 합병증

4-6 Wonderful Buildings

📝 **Grammar Activities**

Type
Pair work / Grammar + Speaking

Aim
To practice passive form with information gap activity

Level
Beginner

Time
10 minutes

Language
Passive form

How to do the activity

1. 수동태를 학습한 뒤 이용할 수 있는 활동입니다.
2. 학생들을 짝 지어 준 뒤 A, B 역할로 나눕니다. A학생에게는 115쪽의 worksheet A를, B학생에게는 116쪽의 worksheet B를 나누어 줍니다. 그리고 절대 서로에게 worksheet을 보여 주지 않도록 합니다.
3. 학생들은 자신이 받은 worksheet에 있는 질문을 상대 학생에게 물어보면서 물음표에 있는 건물이 무엇인지 맞추어야 합니다. 상대 학생은 자신의 worksheet에 주어진 정보를 이용해서 질문에 답을 해 줍니다. 이 때 완벽한 수동태 문장으로 질문에 답을 하도록 합니다.
4. 활동이 끝난 후 어떤 건물인지 정답을 맞추어 보도록 합니다.
5. 117쪽의 정답지를 학생들에게 나누어 주고 수동태를 다시 확인하도록 합니다.

Teacher's Talk

1. I want you to choose a partner and then decide who's going to be "Student A" and who's going to be "Student B." I'm going to give worksheet A to Student A and worksheet B to Student B. Do NOT show your worksheet to your partner. The worksheets have different information on it.
2. Ask the questions from your worksheet to your partner and then write their answers on your worksheet. After writing their answers, guess what kind of building your partner is talking about.
3. When answering the questions, you must use the sentences of passive form.

Ryan's Tip

1. 두 학생이 서로 다른 정보를 확보한 상황에서 과제를 해결하기 위해서 서로의 정보를 공유함으로써 자연스럽게 대화가 발생할 수 있도록 유도하는 활동을 "information gap" 활동이라고 합니다. 영어 말하기 수업에서 가장 보편적으로 사용되는 활동이 이 information gap이라고 할 수 있습니다. information gap 활동에서 중요한 것은 두 학생간의 정보 교류입니다. 간혹 활동을 귀찮아하는 학생들은 서로의 worksheet을 그냥 보여주고 정답을 베끼도록 하는 경우가 있습니다. 이런 경우를 막기 위해서는 instruction을 줄 때 절대로 서로의 worksheet을 보여주지 않도록 미리 주지를 시켜야 하고 또한 활동 중에 교사가 부지런히 학생들을 monitor해야 합니다.

《출처 : 영문법 훈련노트 1 (박용호, 길벗이지톡)》

4-6 Wonderful Buildings

Worksheet A

locate 위치시키다 / *complete* 완성하다 / *emperor* 황제 / *protect* 보호하다 / *enemy* 적 / *purpose* 목적

1. located in India
2. built by Sha Jahan
3. completed in 1653
4. built for the emperor's wife

?

1. Where is it located?
   _____.
2. By whom was it designed?
   _____.
3. When was it built?
   _____.
4. For whom was it built?
   _____.

1. located in China
2. built by Qin Shi Huang
3. completed in 206 BC
4. to protect China from its enemies

?

1. Where is it located?
   _____.
2. By whom was it designed?
   _____.
3. When was it built?
   _____.
4. For what purpose is it used?
   _____.

Grammar Activities

Worksheet B

locate 위치시키다 / *complete* 완성하다 / *emperor* 황제 / *protect* 보호하다 / *enemy* 적 / *purpose* 목적

| ? | 1. Where is it located?
 _____.
 2. By whom was it built?
 _____.
 3. When was it completed?
 _____.
 4. For whom was it built?
 _____. |

1. located in Spain

2. designed by Gaudi

3. completed in 1912

4. built for a rich couple

| ? | 1. Where is it located?
 _____.
 2. By whom was it built?
 _____.
 3. When was it completed?
 _____.
 4. Why was it built?
 _____. |

1. located in Australia

2. built by Utzon

3. built in 1973

4. used for concerts

4-6 Wonderful Buildings

Answers

1. **Where is it located?**
   ➡ It is located in India.
2. **By whom was it built?**
   ➡ It was built by Sha Jahan.
3. **When was it completed?**
   ➡ It was completed in 1653.
4. **For whom was it built?**
   ➡ It was built for the emperor's wife.

1. **Where is it located?**
   ➡ It is located in Spain.
2. **By whom was it built?**
   ➡ It was designed by Gaudi.
3. **When was it completed?**
   ➡ It was completed in 1912.
4. **For whom was it built?**
   ➡ It was built for a rich couple.

1. **Where is it located?**
   ➡ It is located in China.
2. **By whom was it built?**
   ➡ It was built by Qin Shi Huang.
3. **When was it completed?**
   ➡ It was completed in 206 BC.
4. **Why was it built?** ➡ It was built to protect China from its enemies.

1. **Where is it located?**
   ➡ It is located in Australia.
2. **By whom was it built?**
   ➡ It was built by Utzon.
3. **When was it completed?**
   ➡ It was built in 1973.
4. **For whom was it built?**
   ➡ It is used for concerts.

Grammar Activities

4-7 World History Map

Type
Pair work / Grammar + speaking + writing

Aim
To practice past tense using world's history

Level
Beginner ~ pre-intermediate

Time
20 minutes

Language
Past tense

How to do the activity

1. 학생들을 짝 지어 준 뒤 A, B 역할로 나눕니다. A학생에게는 119쪽의 Student A worksheet을, B학생에게는 119쪽의 Student B worksheet을 나누어 줍니다. 그리고 절대 서로에게 worksheet을 보여 주지 않도록 합니다.

2. 학생들은 sample dialog에서 보여주는 것과 같이 대화를 이용해서 자신이 가지고 있는 World History의 빈 칸을 채워야 합니다. 절대로 worksheet을 보여주지 말고 대화를 이용하여 정보를 얻을 수 있도록 합니다.

3. World History 표를 완성 한 뒤 학생들에게 World History를 완성하도록 합니다. World History 표에 나와 있는 정보를 이용해서 각 나라의 빈 칸에 그 나라에서 일어난 과거 역사를 영어 문장으로 쓰도록 합니다.

4. World History 를 완성한 후 교사와 정답을 비교해 봅니다.

Teacher's Talk

1. I want you to choose a partner and then decide who's going to be "Student A" and who's going to be "Student B." I'm going to give worksheet A to Student A and worksheet B to Student B. Do NOT show your worksheet to your partner. The worksheets have different information on it.

2. Ask your partner, "What happened in XXXX?" and then complete the World History Chart with your partner's answers.

3. Using the information from the World History Chart, fill in the blanks on the World History. You should write a full sentence using past tense.

4. (Five minutes later) Let's check the answers together. Sujin, can you tell me what happened in America? (Sujin answers.)

Ryan's Tip

1. 학생들이 활동을 스스로 하는 동안 교사가 할 일은 학생들의 활동을 monitor 하는 것입니다. 만일 과제를 빨리 끝낸 학생들이 있다면 여분의 과제나 어려운 문제를 제공해 주도록 합니다. 반대로 과제를 힘들어하는 학생들에게는 친절한 과외(?)가 필요하겠죠. 또한 학생들의 language error를 기록했다가 활동이 끝나고 난 뒤 feedback 시간에 error correction을 해 주는 것도 필요합니다. 시간이 얼마 남았다는 것을 지속적으로 알려주는 것도 잊지 마세요. 그래야 학생들이 느슨하게 활동에 임하는 것을 막을 수 있습니다.

World History – Student (A)

1. Ask your partner, "What happened in XXXX?" and then complete the chart with your partner's answers.

Sample ▶ A: What happened in **1988**?   B: **Korea hosted the Olympic Games.**

(World History Chart)

Year	World Event	Year	World Event
1492	Columbus / find / America	1988	
1994	Nelson Mandela / become / the President of South Africa	200 BC	
2,500 BC	Egyptian pyramids / be built	1570	
1989	The Communism / fall down in Russia	1911	
1530	The Inca Empire / end	50 BC	

2. Using the World History Chart, write what happened in each country. Make sure to use past tense.

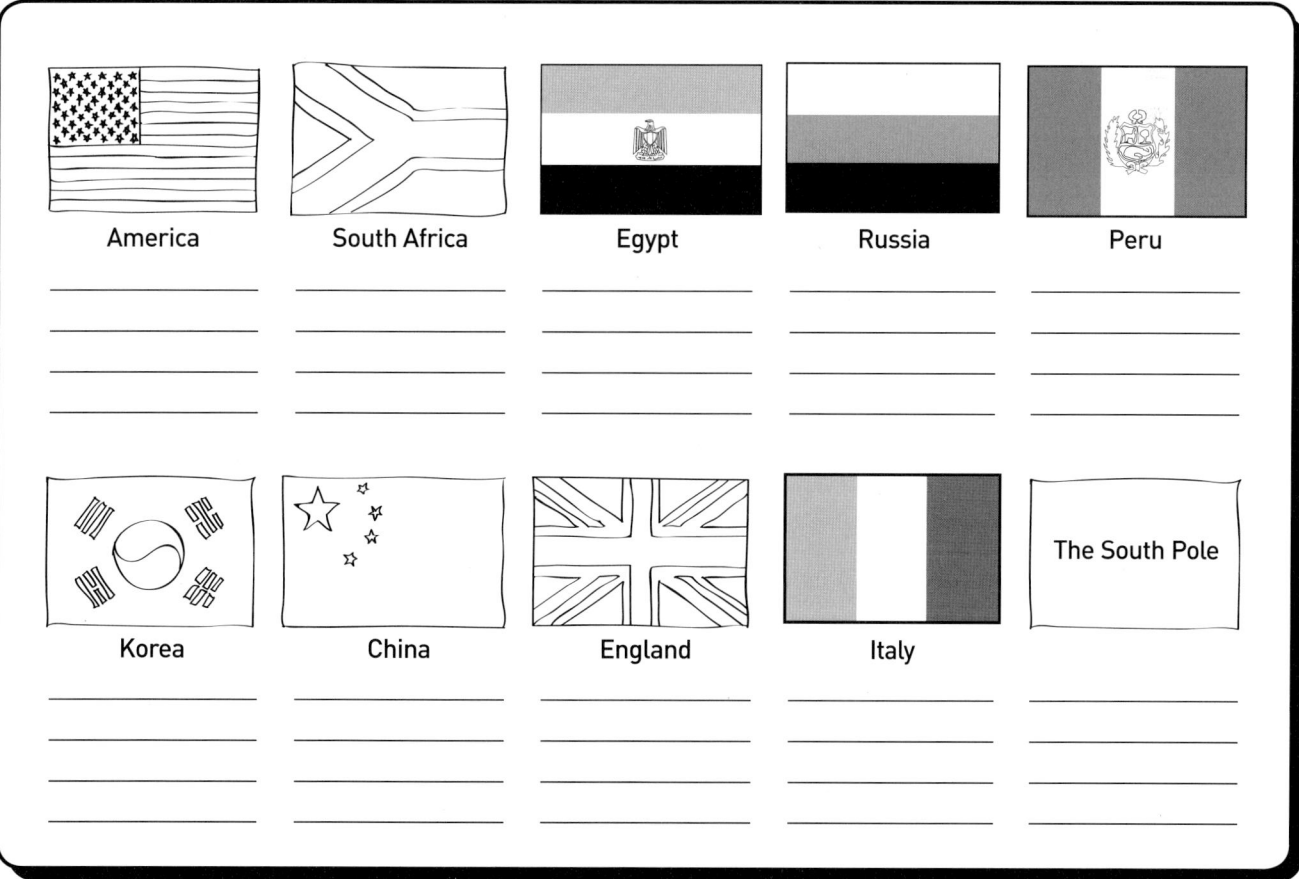

America   South Africa   Egypt   Russia   Peru

Korea   China   England   Italy   The South Pole

 Grammar Activities

World History – Student (B)

1. Ask your partner, "What happened in XXXX?" and then complete the chart with your partner's answer.

Sample ▶ A : What happened in **1492**?   B : **Columbus found America.**

(World History Chart)

Year	World Event	Year	World Event
1492		1988	Korea / host / the Olympic Games
1994		200 BC	Qin dynasty / rule / China
2,500 BC		1570	Elizabeth / rule / England
1989		1911	The South Pole / be found
1530		50 BC	Rome / control / Europe

2. Using the World History Chart, write what happened in each country. Make sure to use past tense.

America   South Africa   Egypt   Russia   Peru

Korea   China   England   Italy   The South Pole

4-7 World History Map

Answers

Using the World History Chart, write what happened in each country. Make sure to use past tense.

USA — Columbus found America in 1492.

South Africa — Nelson Mandela became the President of South Africa in 1994.

Egypt — Egyptian pyramids were built in 2,500 BC.

Russia — The communism fell down in Russia in 1989.

Peru — The Inca Empire ended in 1530.

Korea — Korea hosted the Olympic Games in 1988.

China — Qin dynasty ruled China in 200 BC.

England — Queen Elizabeth ruled England in 1570.

Italy — Rome controlled Europe in 50 BC.

The South Pole — The South Pole was found in 1911.

✂

Answers

Using the World History Chart, write what happened in each country. Make sure to use past tense.

USA — Columbus found America in 1492.

South Africa — Nelson Mandela became the President of South Africa in 1994.

Egypt — Egyptian pyramids were built in 2,500 BC.

Russia — The communism fell down in Russia in 1989.

Peru — The Inca Empire ended in 1530.

Korea — Korea hosted the Olympic Games in 1988.

China — Qin dynasty ruled China in 200 BC.

England — Queen Elizabeth ruled England in 1570.

Italy — Rome controlled Europe in 50 BC.

The South Pole — The South Pole was found in 1911.

4-8 Grammar Auction

📝 **Grammar Activities**

Type
Group work / Grammar review

Aim
To review previous grammar lesson

Level
All level

Time
10 ~ 15 minutes

Language
Grammar review

How to do the activity

1. 한 단원을 배우고 난 뒤 그 단원에서 등장한 문법 사항을 리뷰할 때 사용하는 활동입니다.

2. 6명이 한 모둠을 만들도록 합니다. 각 모둠에 123쪽의 돈을 복사하여 1,000달러씩 나누어 줍니다. 이 돈으로 학생들은 Grammar Auction (문법 경매)에 참여할 수 있습니다.

3. 교사는 경매 진행자로서의 역할을 합니다. 먼저 오늘 문법 경매에 등장할 문법 사항들을 소개합니다. 한 단원에서 배웠던 여러 문법 사항의 타이틀만 약 8~10가지 공개합니다. 대명사, to 부정사, 관계대명사 등으로 제목만 공개합니다. 학생들은 1,000달러를 이용하여 각 문법 사항들을 경매로 살 수 있습니다.

4. 모든 문법 사항에 대한 경매가 다 끝나면 학생들이 문제를 풀도록 합니다. 문제를 구입한 팀이 문제를 풀 수 있는 기회를 먼저 가지게 됩니다. 그 팀이 문제의 정답을 말하면 구입한 금액의 두 배의 금액을 받게 됩니다. 정답을 말하지 못하면 다른 팀에게 문제를 풀 수 있는 기회가 주어지고 돈도 역시 그 팀에게 수여가 됩니다.

5. 문법 문제를 다 풀면 가장 돈을 많이 모은 팀이 승리하게 됩니다.

Teacher's Talk

1. Today, we're going to have a Grammar Auction. First, I want you to make a group of six students.

2. I'm going to give $1,000 to each group. With this money, you're going to buy grammar questions. Here are the titles of the grammar questions. I'm going to give your group two minutes to decide which questions you are going to buy in the auction.

3. (2 minutes later) Welcome to the English Grammar Auction. The first item on sale is a pronoun. Do I hear one hundred dollars? (Continue the auction)

4. Let's solve the questions. The groups who bought questions have a chance to solve those questions first. The group who gives the right answer will get double amount of money that it spent. If the answer is wrong, the other groups will have a chance to solve the question.

Ryan's Tip

1. 문법 문제는 문장을 주고 틀린 부분을 찾는 유형으로 주는 것이 좋습니다. 수준이 높은 학생들은 그것이 왜 틀렸는지 이유를 이야기 하도록 합니다.

《출처 : 2001년 IH in Sydney의 TEFL 과정에서 했던 활동을 응용했습니다.》

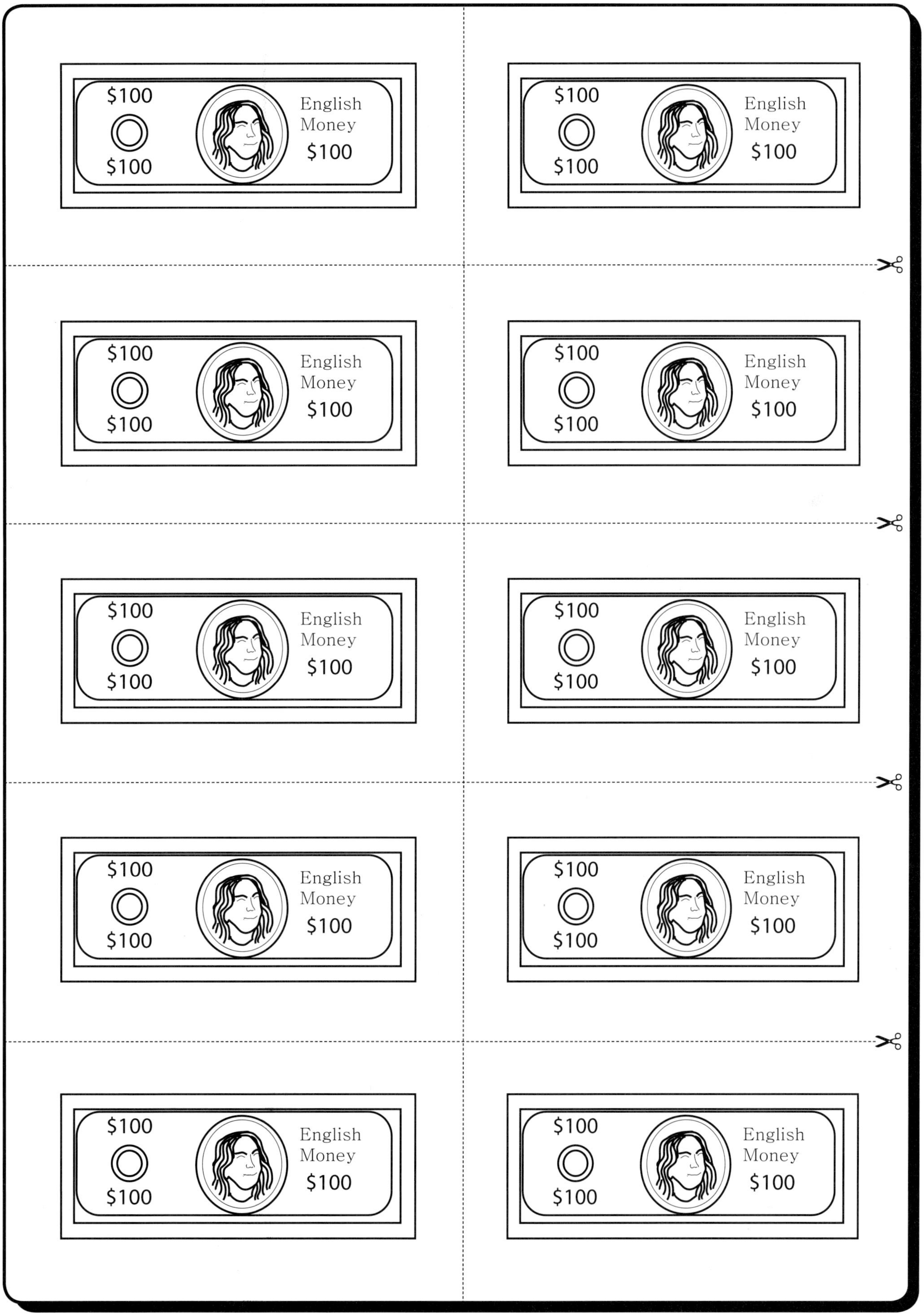

4-8 Grammar Auction

Grammar Activities

4-9 What Will Happen Next?

Type
Pair work / Grammar

Aim
To practice future tense

Level
Beginner

Time
10 ~ 15 minutes

Language
Future tense (possibility)

How to do the activity

1. 미래시제를 공부한 뒤 사용하는 활동입니다. 학생들에게 125쪽의 그림을 잘라 한 장씩 나누어 줍니다.

2. 학생들은 Section A의 그림을 보고 앞으로 무슨 일이 있을지를 추측해서 간단하게 옆의 칸 Section B에 표현하도록 합니다. 그리고 그림의 내용을 밑의 칸에 영어로 작성하도록 합니다. 그림이 완성되면 Section B가 Section A뒤로 위치할 수 있도록 반으로 접도록 합니다.

3. 모든 학생들이 자리에서 일어섭니다. 그리고 다른 학생에게 자신의 Section A를 보여 준 뒤 "What will happen next?"라고 물어봅니다. 그러면 다른 학생은 앞으로 어떤 일이 있을지 자신의 생각을 영어로 말합니다. 이 때 미래시제 will 이나 be going to 를 사용하도록 주지시켜 주세요. 그 후 그림 B를 보여 주면서 정답을 공개해 줍니다. 이 과정을 총 3명의 다른 학생에게 진행하도록 합니다.

Teacher's Talk

1. I'm going to give you a worksheet that has two sections. Section A has a picture of an event and Section B is blank. You need to guess what will happen after the event in Section A and then draw a picture of your prediction in Section B. Also, you need to write a sentence about your picture (in Section B) using the future tense. Lastly, fold the worksheet in half so that you can hide your picture behind Section A.

2. (After students draw their pictures) Now, I want you to stand up and find three different people. Show them your picture in Section A and let them guess what will happen in Section B. After they tell you their guess, show them your drawing in Section B.

Ryan's Tip

1. 재미있는 동영상을 이용하여 앞으로 있을 일을 추측하는 활동을 하는 것도 좋습니다. Youtube 사이트에서 America's Funniest Home Video라는 프로그램을 검색합니다. AFV는 재미있는 홈비디오 장면을 보여주는 프로그램입니다.

2. 재미있는 장면들을 학생들에게 보여주다가 프로그램을 정지(pause)시킵니다. 그리고는 학생들에게 "What will happen next?"라고 물어 본 후 무슨 일이 있을지 생각해 보도록 합니다. 질문을 답할 때는 미래시제를 사용하도록 합니다.

4-9 What Will Happen Next?

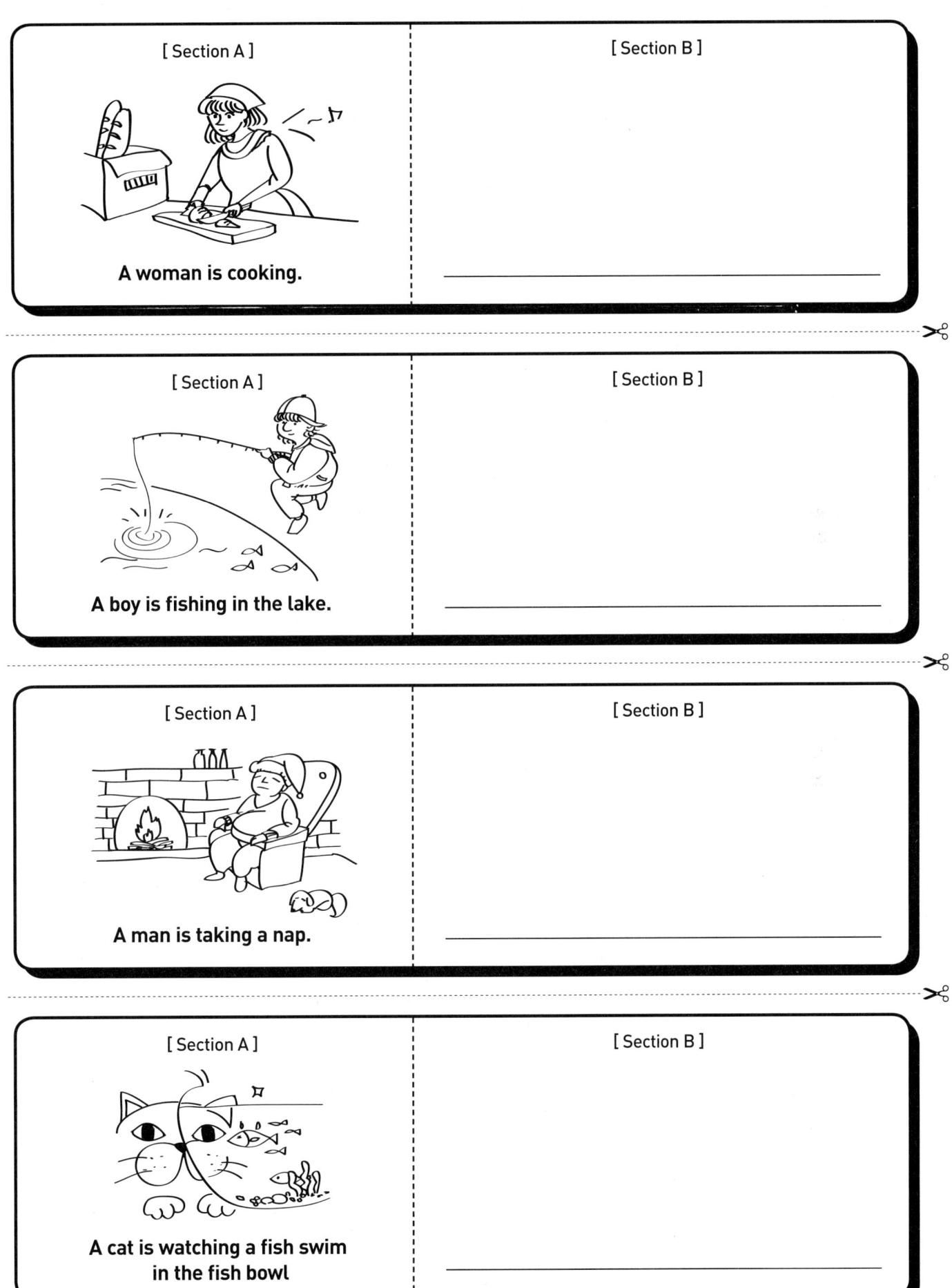

4-10 Grammar Battleship

Type
Group work / Grammar

Aim
To review previous grammar lesson

Level
All level

Time
10 ~ 15 minutes

Language
Grammar review

Grammar Activities

How to do the activity

1. 한 단원을 배우고 난 후 그 단원에서 등장하는 문법사항을 정리할 때 사용하는 활동입니다.
2. 학생들을 두 팀으로 나눈 후 각 팀의 captain 을 뽑도록 합니다.
3. captain에게 127쪽의 표를 잘라서 나누어 줍니다. captain은 표에 5대의 battleship을 배치해야 합니다. 각 battleship의 크기는 정사각형 3칸에 해당하며 표에 수직 혹은 수평으로 배치할 수 있습니다. 절대 대각선으로는 배치할 수 없습니다. battleship 배치가 끝나면 배치된 표를 자신의 팀원들에게만 보여 줍니다. 절대 상대편에게 보여 주어서는 안됩니다.
4. 학생들이 battleship을 배치하는 동안 교사는 각 팀과 동일한 표 2개를 칠판에 크게 그려 둡니다.
5. 교사가 문법적인 오류가 있는 문장을 하나씩 제시하면 학생들은 그 문장에서 문법적으로 어색한 부분을 찾아 바르게 고쳐야 합니다. 가장 빨리 정답을 이야기 하는 학생이 속한 팀은 다른 팀의 battleship을 격침시키기 위해 미사일 5개를 쏠 수 있습니다. 미사일을 쏘는 좌표는 "A5" "C3" 등으로 부릅니다. 만일 그 좌표에 상대편의 battleship이 위치해 있으면 교사가 "Hit" 이라고 말하고 그 좌표에 동그라미를 표시합니다. 만일 좌표에 상대편의 battleship이 없으면 "Miss"라고 이야기 해주고 X 표시를 합니다. 이렇게 battleship이 위치한 3개의 좌표를 정확하게 찾으면 그 배는 좌초하게 됩니다.
6. 이런 식으로 문법 문제를 하나씩 맞출 때마다 그 팀은 5개의 미사일을 쏘게 됩니다. 문법 문제가 모두 끝나면 몇 대의 battleship이 살아 남았나를 계산하고 가장 많은 battleship이 남은 팀이 승리하게 됩니다.

Teacher's Talk

1. Today, we're going to play Grammar Battleship. After I divide the class into two teams, you need to choose a team captain.
2. I'm giving a grid to the team captains. The captains need to place five battleships anywhere on the grid by shading three squares vertically or horizontally for each battleship. You cannot position your battleships diagonally.
3. Now, I'm going to show you sentences with grammatical mistakes. If you know what the mistakes are, shout your team name and correct the mistakes. If you answer correctly, then your captain can call out a grid code (like A5, C3, etc.,) to launch a missile on your opponent's grid. You can launch 5 missiles at a time. If you hit your opponent's battleship, I will say, "Hit" and then I'll circle that position on the grid that I drew on the blackboard. If you miss it, I'll say, "Miss" and then I'll put an "X" on the blackboard. If you hit the three grid codes of your opponent's battleship, you sink it.
4. The team that sinks the most battleships wins the game.

Ryan's Tip

1. 각 팀에서 정답을 맞춘 학생은 다시 정답을 이야기 할 수 없습니다. 다른 학생들의 참여를 유도하기 위해서 입니다.

《출처 : 미국 아이들이 많이 하는 Battleship게임에서 아이디어를 얻었습니다.》

Grammar Battleship Game

Team A : Place 5 battleships (three-square long ships) on the grid.

	1	2	3	4	5	6	7
A							
B							
C							
D							
E							
F							
G							

Grammar Battleship Game

Team B : Place 5 battleships (three-square long ships) on the grid.

	1	2	3	4	5	6	7
A							
B							
C							
D							
E							
F							
G							

UNIT 5

Vocabulary
Activities

UNIT 5 Vocabulary Activities

5-1	What Should I Buy? (p.130 ~ p.133)
Type	Group work
Aim	To practice vocabulary of electric devices
Level	Beginner ~ pre-intermediate
Time	30 minutes

5-2	What Do you Have in Your House? (p.134 ~ p.137)
Type	Pair work
Aim	To practice vocabulary of household objects
Level	Beginner
Time	30 minutes

5-3	New Words in Context (p.138 ~ p.141)
Type	Solo work
Aim	To memorize the meanings of words in context
Level	Beginner
Time	10 ~ 15 minutes

5-4	Cause & Effect of Feeling (p.142 ~ p.143)
Type	Solo work
Aim	To make sentences using words of feeling
Level	Beginner ~ pre-intermediate
Time	20 ~ 25 minutes

5-5	Get Rid of Your Preposition (p.144 ~ p.147)
Type	Group work
Aim	To practice proper use of prepositions
Level	Beginner ~ pre-intermediate
Time	10 ~ 15 minutes

5-6	Life Roadmap (p.148 ~ p.151)
Type	Solo work
Aim	To practice vocabulary about life events
Level	Beginner ~ pre-intermediate
Time	50 minutes

5-7	Order Your Sandwich (p.152 ~ p.155)
Type	Pair work
Aim	To practice ordering a sandwich using food vocabulary
Level	Pre-intermediate ~ intermediate
Time	25 ~ 30 minutes

5-8	Vocabulary Quiz Board Game (p.156 ~ p.157)
Type	Group work
Aim	To test students' vocabulary by playing a board game
Level	All level
Time	30 ~ 40 minutes

5-9	Fix Your Konglish (p.158 ~ p.161)
Type	Group Work
Aim	To learn about improper English expressions (Konglish)
Level	Beginner ~ pre-intermediate
Time	15 ~ 20 minutes

5-10	How Do You Pronounce This Brand? (p.162 ~ p.164)
Type	Solo work
Aim	To practice proper pronunciations
Level	Beginner ~ pre-intermediate
Time	20 ~ 25 minutes + assignment

5-1

🖥️ **Vocabulary Activities**

What Should I Buy?

Type
Group work / Vocabulary

Aim
To practice vocabulary of electric devices

Level
Beginner ~ pre-intermediate

Time
30 minutes

Language
Vocabulary of electric devices or appliances / Numbers

How to do the activity

1. 학생들에게 131쪽의 handout을 잘라서 나누어 줍니다. 학생들은 전자 기기와 그 목적을 알맞게 연결해야 합니다. 하반 학생의 경우에는 전자 기기 단어를 미리 학습하도록 한 뒤 연결하는 활동을 합니다. 교사와 함께 정답을 확인해 봅니다. 이 외에도 다른 전자 기기는 어떻게 읽는지 학습합니다.

2. 4~5명의 학생이 한 모둠이 됩니다.

3. 각 모둠에 132쪽의 전자기기 카드를 잘라 나누어 줍니다. 학생들이 책상위에 카드를 골고루 펴놓도록 합니다.

4. 각 모둠에서 Reader 한 명을 선정합니다. 교사는 Reader에게 133쪽에 있는 질문지를 나누어 주고 절대 다른 학생에게 보여 주지 않도록 합니다.

5. Reader가 질문을 읽으면 학생들은 그 질문에 맞는 전자기기 카드를 재빨리 집고 그 기기의 영어 단어를 말해야 합니다. 정확하게 단어를 발음하면 그 카드를 소유할 수 있습니다. 만일 시간 내로 말하지 못하거나 정확하지 않으면 다른 학생에게 기회가 있습니다.

6. Reader의 질문이 끝난 후 가장 많은 카드를 소유한 학생이 승리하게 됩니다.

Teacher's Talk

1. I'm going to give you a handout. Match the electric devices with the right purposes. (3 minutes later) Now, let's check the answers.

2. Make groups of five students and then choose a group reader.

3. I'm going to give you a deck of cards with the name of electric devices on them. Spread the cards face up on the table.

4. Readers, your job is to read the questions to your group members. Group members, listen to each question carefully, pick up the correct card, and say the electric device in English. If you fail to say the exact word, you have to put the card back, and someone else in your team will have a chance to say the word. If you succeed, you can keep the card.

5. We'll play this game until the reader runs out of questions. The student who collects the most cards will be the winner.

Ryan's Tip

1. 각 단어 밑에 가격을 적어 두었습니다. 하반 수업에서 숫자 읽기 학습으로 이 카드를 재활용하실 수 있습니다.

5-1 What Should I Buy?

*Match the electric devices with the right purposes.

Devices	Purposes
vacuum cleaner	to keep my soda cool
electronic dictionary	to wake up on time
laptop	to watch my favorite show
humidifier	to iron my shirts
TV	to do laundry
iron	to clean up my room
hair dryer	to dry my hair
refrigerator	to read English books
alarm clock	to check my email
washing machine	to keep my room humid

---

*Match the electric devices with the right purposes.

Devices	Purposes
vacuum cleaner	to keep my soda cool
electronic dictionary	to wake up on time
laptop	to watch my favorite show
humidifier	to iron my shirts
TV	to do laundry
iron	to clean up my room
hair dryer	to dry my hair
refrigerator	to read English books
alarm clock	to check my email
washing machine	to keep my room humid

Vocabulary Activities

laptop
(698,000 won)

digital camera
(359,430 won)

electronic dictionary
(215,420 won)

cell phone
(294,870 won)

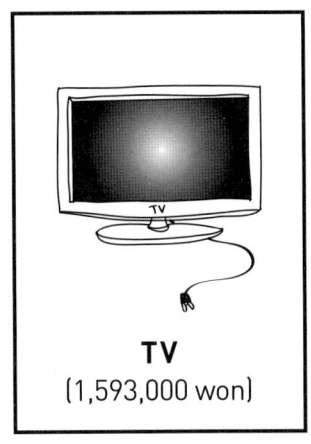
TV
(1,593,000 won)

refrigerator
(1,342,000 won)

washing machine
(817,440 won)

humidifier
(53,600 won)

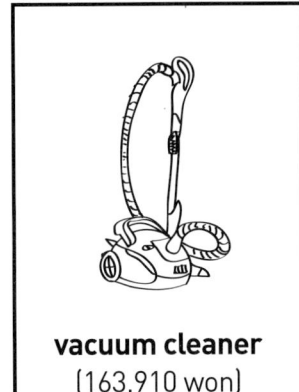
vacuum cleaner
(163,910 won)

iron
(99,870 won)

hair dryer
(77,770 won)

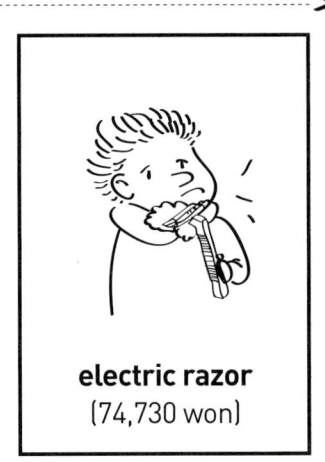
electric razor
(74,730 won)

alarm clock
(15,480 won)

oven
(450,000 won)

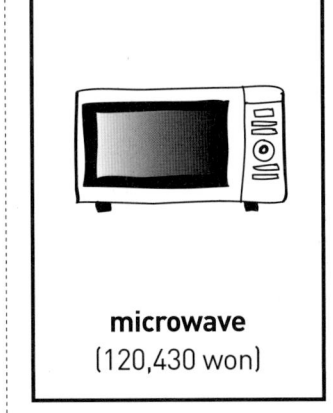
microwave
(120,430 won)

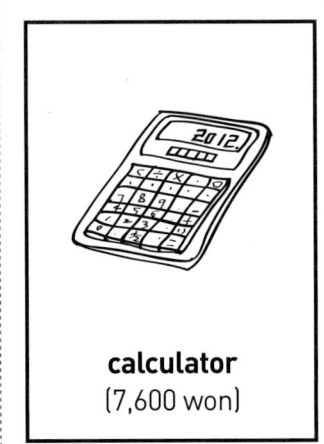
calculator
(7,600 won)

5-1 What Should I Buy?

*Readers! Read the following questions to your team members.

Q1 I want to keep my soda cool all day long. What should I buy?
A1 Refrigerator

Q2 My room is so dry. What should I buy?
A2 Humidifier

Q3 I want to check my email at home. What should I buy?
A3 Laptop

Q4 I want to read English books but I don't know many words. What should I buy?
A4 Electronic dictionary

Q5 It takes so long to dry my hair with a towel. What should I buy?
A5 Hair dryer

Q6 I was late for work again. I need to get up on time. What should I buy?
A6 Alarm clock

Q7 My room is so dusty. I need to clean up my room. What should I buy?
A7 Vacuum cleaner

Q8 I need to do laundry. What should I buy?
A8 Washing machine

Q9 I want to watch my favorite show. What should I buy?
A9 TV

Q10 I want to iron my shirts. What should I buy?
A10 Iron

5-2

🖥️ **Vocabulary Activities**

What Do You Have in Your House?

Type
Pair work / Vocabulary

Aim
To practice vocabulary of household objects

Level
Beginner

Time
30 minutes

Language
Vocabulary of household objects / Do you have ~?

How to do the activity

1. 학생들에게 135쪽의 worksheet을 나누어 줍니다.
2. 학생들과 household object를 학습합니다. 발음을 학습한 뒤 그 뜻을 빈칸에 적도록 합니다.
3. 두 학생이 한 조가 되도록 짝을 만듭니다. 학생들은 136쪽의 worksheet에 나와 있는 4개의 장소인 bathroom, bedroom, kitchen, living room에 자신의 집에서 볼 수 있는 household object 를 5개씩 적어야 합니다. 절대로 짝에게 자신이 적은 단어를 보여 주어서는 안 됩니다.
4. worksheet에 단어를 쓰는 일이 끝나면 짝의 집안 물건과 나의 집안 물건 중 일치하는 것을 찾고 동그라미 치도록 합니다. 일치하는 것을 찾을 때는 다음과 같은 짧은 대화를 이용하도록 합니다.
　　A : Do you have a bathtub in your bathroom?
　　B : Yes, I do. / No, I don't.
5. 일치하는 물건의 개수를 worksheet 맨 아래에 적도록 합니다.

Teacher's Talk

1. Today, we're going to learn some words about household objects. I'm going to give you a worksheet containing 40 words of household objects. Let's practice how to say the words. (After pronunciation drill) Now, I'm going to tell you the meaning of each word. Write it down in the parenthesis.
2. On the second worksheet, there is a house with four rooms; a bathroom, a bedroom (your bedroom), a kitchen and a living room. In the blanks of each room, you need to write five household objects that you have in your house. You can use the words that we've just learned. Do NOT show your worksheet to your partner.
3. Now, let's compare what you have in your house with your partner. Using the sample dialog, try to find what household objects you and your partner have in common. If you find the same objects, circle them. Write down the number of the same household objects at the bottom of the worksheet. Why don't we take a look at the sample dialog before we start?

Ryan's Tip

1. 시간의 여유가 있다면 136쪽의 worksheet을 나누어 주기 전에 집에 어떤 물건이 있는지 학생들에게 elicit 할 수 있습니다.

5-2 What Do You Have in Your House?

A. Let's practice the words of household objects.
Write the Korean meanings of the words in the blanks.

Living room	Kitchen	My room	Bathroom
sofa / couch ( )	sink ( )	curtains ( )	mirror ( )
television ( )	refrigerator ( )	rug ( )	medicine cabinet ( )
coffee table ( )	cabinet ( )	bed ( )	toilet ( )
stereo system ( )	stove ( )	lamp ( )	towel ( )
carpet ( )	microwave ( )	pillow ( )	toothbrush holder ( )
book shelf ( )	toaster ( )	drawer ( )	faucet ( )
DVD player ( )	blender ( )	wardrobe ( )	bathtub ( )
painting ( )	table ( )	desk ( )	toilet paper ( )
floor light ( )	chair ( )	radio ( )	toilet plunger ( )
air conditioner ( )	dish washer ( )	alarm clock ( )	magnifying mirror ( )

라이언 쌤, 이렇게 가르쳐서 영어수업 대박내다 Ⅱ - **활동편** 135

Vocabulary Activities

B. Write five household objects that you have in your house.

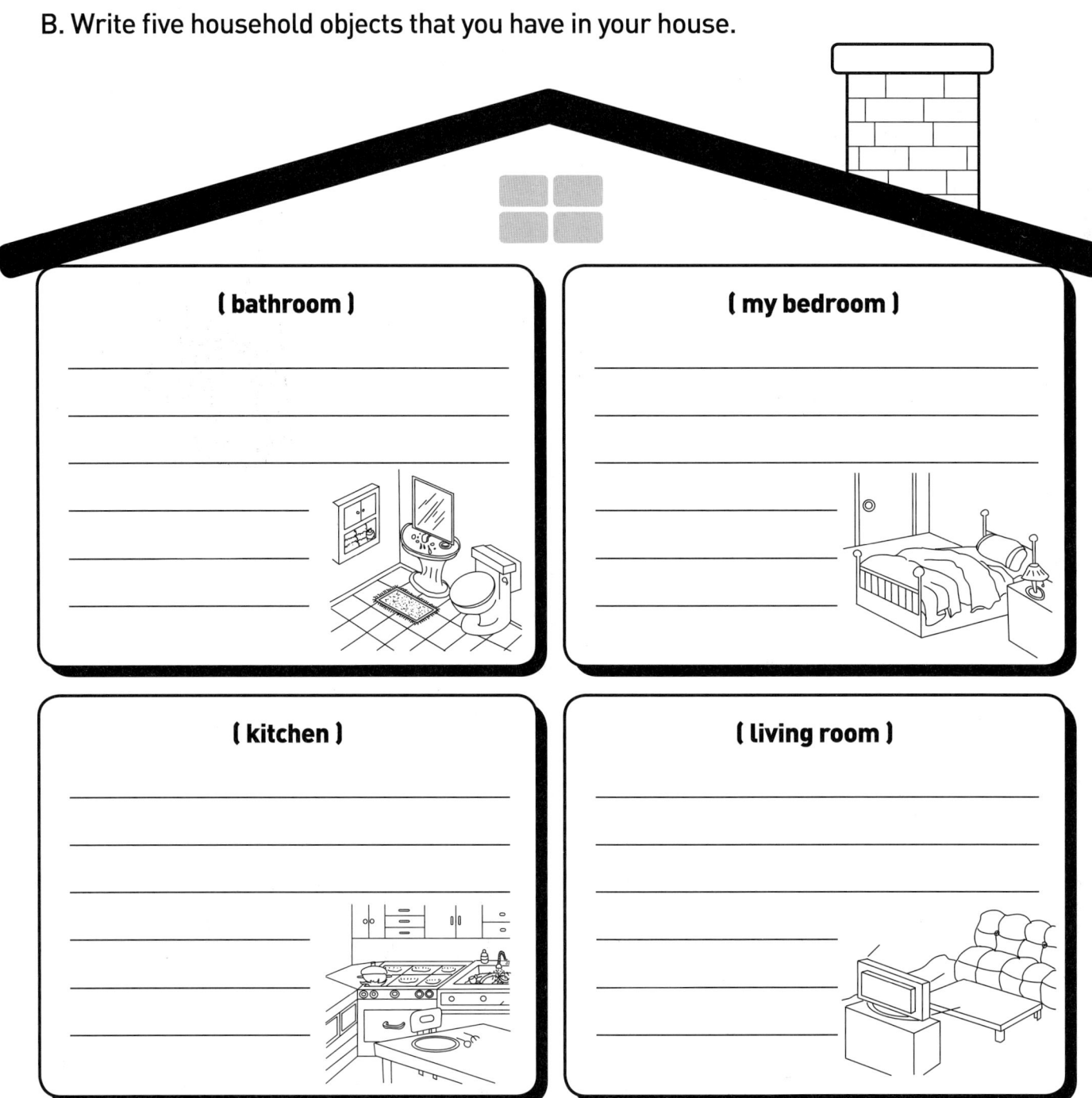

C. Compare what you've written with your partner.
Using the dialog below, find out what kind of household objects you and your partner have in common. If you find the same objects, circle them.

(Sample Dialog)
A : Do you have a **bathtub** in your **bathroom**?
B : Yes, I do. / No, I don't.

How many household objects do you and your partner have in common? (   )

5-2 What Do You Have in Your House?

Let's Take a Quiz

Write appropriate Korean meanings in the blank.

Living room	Kitchen	My room	Bathroom
sofa / couch ( )	sink ( )	curtains ( )	mirror ( )
television ( )	refrigerator ( )	rug ( )	medicine cabinet ( )
coffee table ( )	cabinet ( )	bed ( )	toilet ( )
stereo system ( )	stove ( )	lamp ( )	towel ( )
carpet ( )	microwave ( )	pillow ( )	toothbrush holder ( )
book shelf ( )	toaster ( )	drawer ( )	faucet ( )
DVD player ( )	blender ( )	wardrobe ( )	bathtub ( )
painting ( )	table ( )	desk ( )	toilet paper ( )
floor light ( )	chair ( )	radio ( )	toilet plunger ( )
air conditioner ( )	dish washer ( )	alarm clock ( )	magnifying mirror ( )

라이언 쌤, 이렇게 가르쳐서 영어수업 대박내다 II - **활동편**

5-3 New Words in Context

Vocabulary Activities

Type
Solo work / Vocabulary

Aim
To memorize the meanings of words in context

Level
Beginner

Time
10 ~ 15 minutes

Language
Vocabulary

How to do the activity

1. 수업에 들어가기 전, 학생들이 배울 새로운 단어와 그 뜻을 유추할 수 있는 한글 문장을 이용하여 139쪽과 동일한 worksheet을 만듭니다. 한글 문장은 그 단어의 뜻이 가장 잘 추측될 수 있도록 만드는 것이 좋습니다.
2. 학생들에게 worksheet을 나누어 준 뒤 한글 문장을 바탕으로 영어 단어의 뜻을 추측, 빈칸에 적도록 합니다.
3. 교사와 함께 단어의 정확한 뜻과 발음을 학습합니다. 3~5분의 시간을 주어 학생들이 단어의 뜻을 그 자리에서 암기할 수 있도록 합니다. 그 후 간단한 퀴즈를 치르도록 합니다.

Teacher's Talk

1. On the worksheet, you'll see the new words that you're going to learn today. Try to guess their meanings by reading the Korean sentences with the new words. Write down the meaning in the blanks. I'll give you 2 minutes.
2. Let's find out the meanings of the words. Kisu, what do you think the meaning of the first word is? ... (After pronunciation drill) Now, you need to memorize the words as well as their meanings. We're going to have a quiz in five minutes.

Ryan's Tip

1. 문맥속에서 단어를 암기하면 좀 더 오랫동안 기억에 남을 수 있습니다. 또한 단어와 뜻만 수동적으로 암기하는 것보다 문맥을 통해서 단어의 뜻을 유추하는 과정을 거치게 되면 재미의 요소도 가미될 수 있습니다.
2. 교과서에 있는 단어들을 이와 같이 구성하여 하나의 단어집을 만들 수도 있습니다. 각 학생들에게 교과서에 등장하는 모든 단어 (교과서 뒷쪽에 나오는 부록 단어면 좋습니다)를 공평하게 배분해 줍니다. 그리고는 학생들이 139쪽과 같이 단어의 뜻을 가장 잘 유추할 수 있는 문장을 만들어 오도록 합니다. 학생들이 만든 worksheet을 수합하여 묶으면 문맥을 이용한 교과서 단어집이 완성됩니다.
3. 141쪽에 감정과 관련된 단어 수업에서 사용하실 수 있도록 worksheet을 만들어 두었습니다.

New Words in Context

Read the Korean sentences and then guess the meanings of the words.
Write them down in the table.

Word	Sentence	Meaning
health	**health**를 유지하려면 규칙적으로 운동을 해야 해.	
improve	영어 실력을 **improve** 하기 위해서는 책을 많이 읽는 것이 좋아	
infection	바이러스 **infection** 때문에 내 컴퓨터가 완전히 고장 나 버렸어.	
expand	풍선이 너무 빨리 **expand** 해 버리더니 결국에는 터져 버렸지 뭐야.	
sweet potato	나는 감자 보다는 **sweet potato**가 더 좋아. 특히 김치와 같이 먹으면 더 맛있지.	
ingredient	요리 **ingredient** 만 가져와. 내가 우리 집에서 맛있는 저녁 식사를 만들어 줄게.	
stir	소스가 냄비에 눌러 붙지 않도록 계속 주걱으로 **stir** 해 주어야 해.	
cough	감기에 걸려서 계속 **cough** 하고 있어요. 내일 병원에 가야겠어요.	
ashamed	무대에서 춤을 추는데 갑자기 의상이 흘러 내렸어요. 너무 **ashamed** 해서 얼굴이 빨개졌죠.	
drought	심각한 **drought**로 농작물이 말라 버렸어요. 큰 우물이라도 찾아 봐야겠어요.	
damage	교통사고로 뇌에 심각한 **damage**를 입었어요. 그래서 반신 불구가 되었죠.	
vehicle	저 차를 몰고 가는 범인을 잡아야 해. 빨리 **vehicle** 한 대를 구해봐.	
distance	**distance**가 너무 멀어서 3시간 만에 거기까지 갈 수는 없다고요.	

📺 **Vocabulary Activities**

New Words in Context

1. Make a Korean sentence using the English word.
Try to make the best sentence to let your partner guess the meaning of the word.

Word	Sentence	Meaning
(example) **delighted**	친구가 손수 만든 필통을 생일 선물로 줘서 너무 **delighted** 했어.	

2. After making the sentences, give this handout to your partner.
Ask your partner to guess the meaning of the word and write it down in the table.

Let's study feeling words

Read the Korean sentences and then guess the meanings of the words.
Write them down in the table.

Word	Sentence	Meaning
anxious	내일 우리 동네에서 슈퍼 콘서트가 열려. 나 너무 **anxious** 해서 잠을 못 자겠어.	
amused	반지를 보자 그 여자는 너무 **amused** 해서 눈물을 흘렸어.	
ashamed	엄마한테 거짓말한 게 들통나서 너무 **ashamed** 해.	
confused	그애의 마음은 너무 이랬다 저랬다 한다구. 난 정말 **confused** 해.	
delighted	우리 학교 축구부가 결승에 진출해서 너무 **delighted** 해.	
excited	내일 너의 생일 파티에 가게 되어서 **excited** 하다구.	
frustrated	시험지를 받았는데 하나도 모르겠는거야. 정말 **frustrated** 했어.	
horrified	혼자 시골길을 걸으면서 그녀는 **horrified** 했을 거야.	
jealous	난 네가 다른 애하고 있으면 정말 너무 **jealous** 해서 미칠 지경이야.	
nervous	너무 **nervous**해서 무대에서 한 걸음도 못 떼겠더라구.	
perplexed	그 사고가 난 곳에서 어떻게 해야 할지 정말 **perplexed** 했지.	
shy	그 애는 여자애들한테 말도 한마디 못 꺼내. 정말 **shy** 하거든.	
terrified	수많은 관중들 앞에서 **terrified** 되어서 목소리가 하나도 안 나왔어.	

5-4

📺 **Vocabulary Activities**

Cause & Effect of Feeling

Type
Solo work / Vocabulary

Aim
To make sentences using words of feeling

Level
Beginner ~ pre-intermediate

Time
20 ~ 25 minutes

Language
Feeling words / because ~

How to do the activity

1. 학생들에게 feeling words를 positive 한 것과 negative 한 것으로 나누어서 eliciting 합니다. 만일 학생들이 143쪽에 등장하는 feeling words를 이야기 하지 않으면 교사가 보충해서 가르치도록 합니다.

2. 학생들에게 143쪽의 worksheet을 나누어 줍니다. 학생들은 feeling words가 들어간 target sentence를 이용하여 예문과 같이 두 개의 문장을 만들어야 합니다. 이 때 접속사 because를 이용하여 그 감정이 왜 생겼는지에 대한 원인 문장을 하나 만들고, 또한 그 감정으로 인해서 어떤 결과가 생겼는지 결과 문장을 하나 만들도록 합니다.

3. 완성된 문장을 짝과 비교해 보고 상대방의 문장 중 가장 재미있는 것 하나를 선정하도록 합니다.

Teacher's Talk

1. Okay, class, can you tell me some "feeling" words that you know? First, tell me some positive "feeling" words such as happy and glad. (Students say some words and the teacher writes them on the board.) Good. Let's move on to negative "feeling" words.

2. Now, I'm going to give you a worksheet. You'll see six short sentences with the "feeling" words that you've just learned. You need to make two other sentences related to the target sentences. Take a look at the sample. As the sample shows, you need to make two sentences using the word "because". I'll give you 10 minutes to complete your sentences.

3. Okay, exchange your worksheet with your partner. Read your partner's sentences and choose the sentence with the most interesting idea.

Ryan's Tip

1. positive feeling words와 negative feeling words를 eliciting 할 때 학생들에게 그 뜻도 말하도록 유도합니다.

2. 영어 수준이 낮은 학생들도 elicit 하도록 하지만 교사가 추가로 feeling words를 제시해 주고 pronunciation drill 까지도 시키도록 합니다.

Cause & Effect of Feeling

(Sample) I'm tired

Because I've been studying all day, I'm tired.
Because I'm tired, I'm going to take a short nap.

---

1. I'm depressed

Because _____, I'm depressed.
Because I'm depressed, _____.

---

2. I was frustrated

Because _____, I was frustrated.
Because I was frustrated, _____.

---

3. I was delighted

Because _____, I was delighted.
Because I was delighted, _____.

---

4. I'm annoyed

Because _____, I'm annoyed.
Because I'm annoyed, _____.

---

5. I'm disappointed

Because _____, I'm disappointed.
Because I'm disappointed, _____.

---

6. I was worried

Because _____, I was worried.
Because I was worried, _____.

5-5 Get Rid of Your Preposition

🖥️ **Vocabulary Activities**

Type
Group work / Vocabulary

Aim
To practice proper use of prepositions

Level
Beginner ~ pre-intermediate

Time
10 ~ 15 minutes

Language
Prepositions

How to do the activity

1. 4~5명의 학생이 한 모둠을 만듭니다. 게임의 진행자를 한 명 선정합니다. 모둠 중에서 영어를 제일 잘하는 학생을 게임의 진행자로 선정하는 것이 좋습니다.

2. 진행자는 모둠의 학생들에게 145~146쪽에서 자른 전치사 카드를 4장씩 나누어 줍니다. 나머지 카드는 책상에 모아 둡니다.

3. 진행자는 147쪽의 문제를 읽어 줍니다. 전치사가 들어가야 하는 빈칸은 "삐리리" 라고 읽습니다. 학생들은 진행자의 문장을 잘 듣고 빈칸에 들어갈 전치사 카드를 가지고 있으면 재빨리 탁자 위에 그 카드를 내려 놓습니다. 가장 빨리 카드를 내려 놓은 학생 한 명만이 그 카드를 자신의 손에서 없앨 수 있습니다. 이렇게 해서 가장 빨리 자신의 손에서 카드를 없애는 학생이 승리합니다.

4. 만일 내려 놓은 카드가 정답이 아니면 오히려 전치사 카드를 한 장 더 받아야 합니다. 신중하게 정답을 생각해야 합니다.

5. Joker card는 어떤 전치사로도 사용될 수 있습니다. 만일 정답이 from인데 from이라는 카드가 없으면 Joker card를 탁자에 놓고 from이라고 외치면 됩니다.

Teacher's Talk

1. Let's make groups of five students. Now, choose a student to host the game in your group.

2. Your host will give four preposition cards to each student. Don't show your cards to each other. Your host will then read sentences containing blanks. If you have the proper preposition card for the blank, put it down on the table quickly. The person who puts it down first can get rid of the card. The purpose of the game is to get rid of all the cards in your hand.

3. If you put down the wrong preposition card, you have to take another preposition card from the pile of cards. Therefore, you should be careful before putting a card down on the table.

4. The Joker card can be any preposition. For example, if you think the answer is *from*, your joker card can be *from*. If you want to use the Joker card, just put it down on the table and say the right answer.

Ryan's Tip

1. card game과 같이 규칙이 복잡한 게임은 말로만 설명하는 것보다 직접 시범을 보이면서 설명하는 demonstration이 효과적입니다.

2. 영어 수준이 낮은 학생들의 경우 전치사의 용법을 설명하고 난 뒤 연습문제 활동으로 하시면 좋습니다.

5-5 Get Rid of Your Preposition

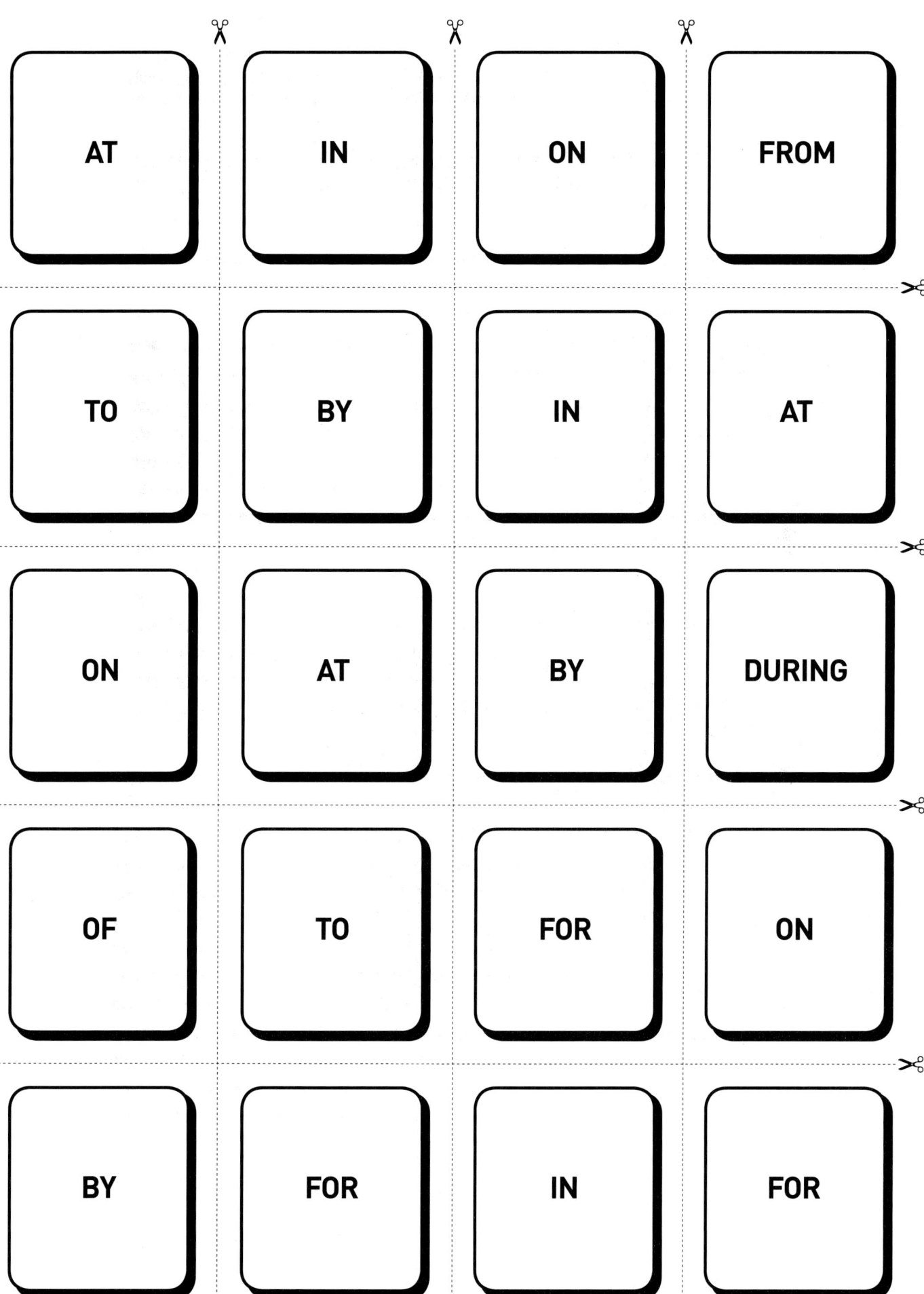

Vocabulary Activities

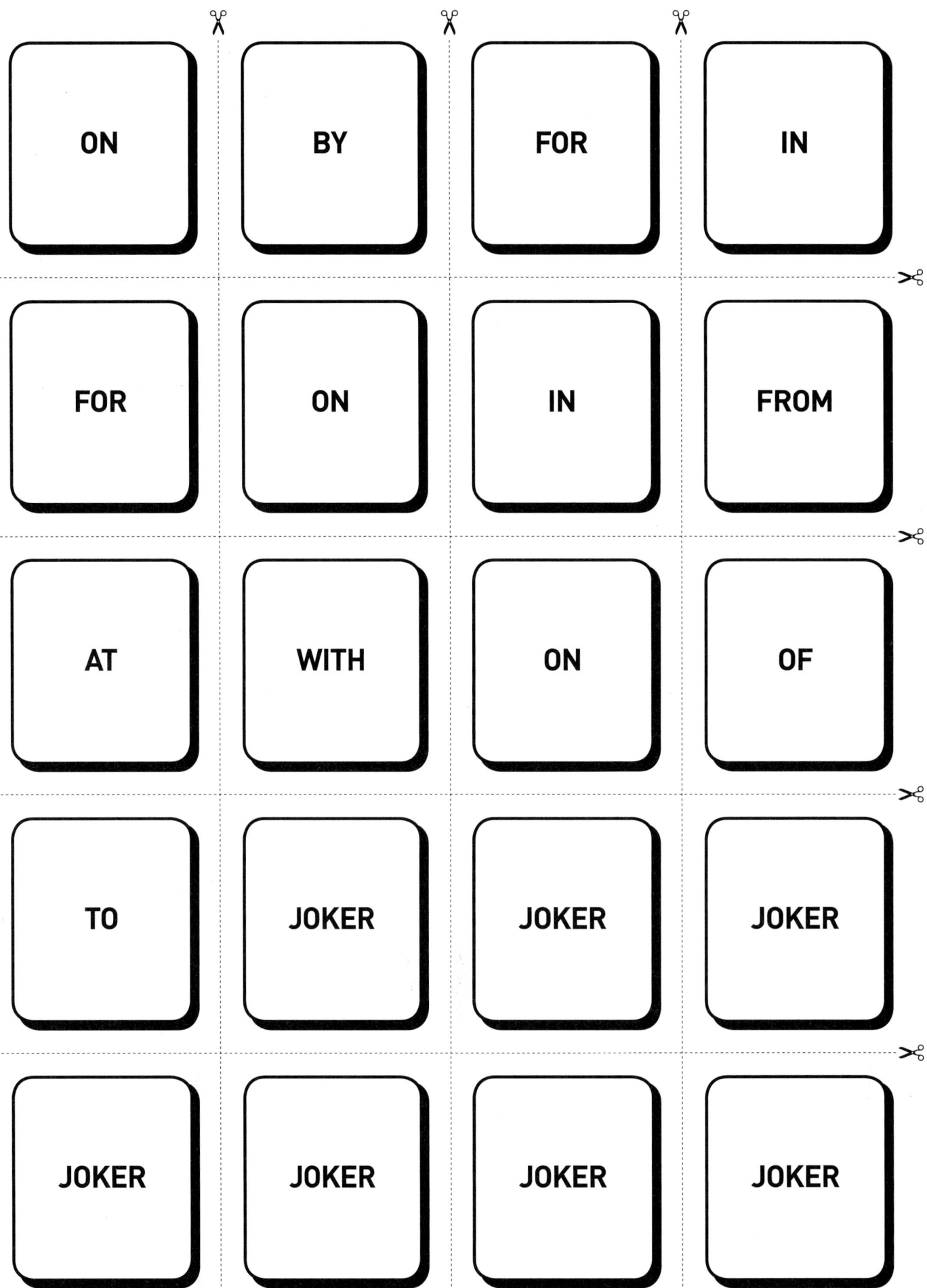

Get Rid of Your Preposition

Read the following sentences to your friends. You can say, "beep" for the blanks.

1.	I go to bed (**at**) 10 p.m.
2.	I always drink milk (**in**) the morning.
3.	My dad comes home late (**on**) Fridays.
4.	We'll go to the concert (**on**) Christmas day.
5.	I have lived in Canada (**for**) five years.
6.	I love to watch movies (**at**) home.
7.	She became the president (**in**) 2009.
8.	Seoul is the capital (**of**) Korea.
9.	Let's go (**to**) the movie tomorrow.
10.	I made the pie (**with**) Susan. She was a good cook.
11.	I am (**from**) Korea. I was born in Seoul.
12.	Look at the picture (**on**) the wall.
13.	You need to talk (**to**) your homeroom teacher.
14.	What do you think (**of**) the project?
15.	There were many people (**at**) the party.
16.	Thank you (**for**) giving the money.
17.	Don't play (**with**) the knife.
18.	We are going to leave the country (**in**) December.
19.	What did you do (**from**) 10 to 11 pm last night?
20.	I visited my friend in Canada (**during**) my vacation.
21.	She was standing (**by**) the building.
22.	I promise that I'll do everything (**for**) you.
23.	She learned English (**by**) watching American movies.
24.	She didn't say anything at all (**during**) the meeting.
25.	My baby needs to take a nap (**in**) the afternoon.
26.	My dad and I play tennis (**on**) weekends.
27.	She spilt coffee (**on**) my book.
28.	I'm going to send a postcard (**to**) my mom.
29.	She's waiting for the bus (**at**) the bus stop.
30.	The book was written (**by**) my best friend.

5-6

💻 Vocabulary Activities

Life Roadmap

Type
Solo work / Vocabulary + Writing

Aim
To practice vocabulary about life events

Level
Beginner ~ pre-intermediate

Time
50 minutes

Language
1. Vocabulary about life events
2. Future tense / past tense

How to do the activity

1. 학생들에게 2분 정도의 시간을 주고 우리의 삶에서 일어 날 수 있는 일들이나 꼭 해야 하는 일들을 생각하도록 합니다. 먼저 교사가 몇 가지 중요한 일들을 말해 주는 것이 좋습니다. (e.g. be born, go to kindergarten, die, etc)

2. elicit을 통해서 학생들이 자신의 생각을 말하도록 합니다. 학생들이 말하는 단어들을 칠판에 적어도 됩니다.

3. 149쪽의 handout을 잘라 나누어 준 뒤, 표현을 다시 익히도록 합니다.

4. 150~151쪽의 Life roadmap을 학생 모두에게 제시합니다. 앞서 나누어 준 life events들이 자신에게 언제 일어날지, 그리고 어떻게 일어날 지 roadmap에 표시하도록 합니다. 교사가 직접 자신이 작성한 roadmap을 샘플로 제시해도 됩니다. 시간은 25분 정도를 주도록 합니다.

5. 작성이 끝나면 짝에게 자신의 roadmap을 소개하도록 합니다. 이 때 이미 일어난 일들은 과거 시제를, 앞으로 일어날 일은 미래 시제를 쓰도록 합니다.

Teacher's Talk

1. Let's think about some common life events that most of us experience in life. For example, we're all born, and most of us go to kindergarten. I'll give you two minutes to think about other major life events.

2. (Two minutes later) Okay, who can tell me some major life events? (Teacher writes them on the board.)

3. I'm going to give you a worksheet. You'll see the list of life events that we just talked about. On the other worksheet, you'll see a road called, "Life Roadmap." I want you to draw your own Life Roadmap with your major life events and your age. For example, if you want to put "get a job" on the road map, you also need to write what kind of job and at what age you'll get the job. Make sure you use most of the life events on the worksheet. If you want, you can add extra life events. I'll give you 25 minutes to complete your road map.

4. Now, compare and explain your road map to your partner.

Ryan's Tip

1. 자신이 작성한 roadmap을 제대로 따르기 위해 지금 자신이 해야 할 일을 생각하고 간단하게 작문하는 활동을 하는 것도 좋습니다.

5-6 Life Roadmap

Let's think about the meanings of the following life events. Also, write down other life events.

be born ( )	go to school ( )	graduate ( )	go to college ( )
join the army ( )	have a boy/girlfriend ( )	get a job ( )	get promoted ( )
buy a house ( )	get married ( )	have a baby ( )	buy a car ( )
travel ( )	retire ( )	have a grandchild ( )	die ( )
(your idea) _____ ( )	(your idea) _____ ( )	(your idea) _____ ( )	(your idea) _____ ( )

✂---

Let's think about the meanings of the following life events. Also, write down other life events.

be born ( )	go to school ( )	graduate ( )	go to college ( )
join the army ( )	have a boy/girlfriend ( )	get a job ( )	get promoted ( )
buy a house ( )	get married ( )	have a baby ( )	buy a car ( )
travel ( )	retire ( )	have a grandchild ( )	die ( )
(your idea) _____ ( )	(your idea) _____ ( )	(your idea) _____ ( )	(your idea) _____ ( )

Vocabulary Activities

I was born in _____.

I went to kindergarten at _____.

_____'s **Life Roadmap**

5-6 Life Roadmap

I'll be in heaven at _____.

5-7

💻 Vocabulary Activities

Order Your Sandwich

Type
Pair work / Vocabulary + Speaking

Aim
To practice ordering a sandwich using food vocabulary

Level
Pre-intermediate ~ intermediate

Time
25 ~ 30 minutes

Language
Food vocabulary / Ordering

How to do the activity

1. 학생들에게 미국에서 가장 흔하게 볼 수 있는 샌드위치 가게 Subway에서 주문하는 방법이 담긴 동영상을 보여 줍니다. 동영상은 인터넷에서 쉽게 찾을 수 있습니다.

2. 학생 2명이 한 조가 되어 한 학생은 샌드위치를 주문하는 역할을, 다른 학생은 주문을 받는 역할을 합니다. 학생들에게 153쪽의 worksheet을 잘라서 나누어 줍니다. 학생들과 worksheet을 보면서 음식과 관련된 단어도 학습하고, 어떻게 샌드위치를 주문하는지를 익히도록 합니다.

3. 교사와의 학습이 끝났으면 주문을 하는 학생이 자신의 샌드위치에 무엇을 넣을지를 생각하고 worksheet에 표시하도록 합니다. 이 때 절대로 주문 받는 학생에게 worksheet을 보여 주어서는 안됩니다.

4. 주문 받는 학생이 "Hi, what would you like?" 라고 물어 보면 샌드위치 주문이 시작됩니다. 주문 받는 학생은 주문 하는 학생이 불러주는 대로 자신의 worksheet에 해당 항목들을 체크해야 합니다. 주문 시에는 154쪽에 주어진 샘플 대화를 이용하도록 합니다.

5. 주문이 다 끝났으면 주문한 샌드위치의 가격이 얼마인지 말해 줍니다. 서로의 worksheet을 같이 공유하면서 주문이 제대로 이루어졌는지 확인합니다.

Teacher's Talk

1. I'm going to show you a short video clip on how to order a sandwich in the US.

2. Now, I'm going to put you in pairs. One of you will order a sandwich while the other one takes the order. Here's a sandwich order form. Let's take a look at the form together.

3. (After teaching vocabulary and how to order) Now, customers, you need to decide what kind of sandwich you want to order by placing check marks on the order form. Start with your choice of bread and then move on to meat, cheese, vegetable, etc. Do NOT show your order form to your partner. I'll give you three minutes.

4. (Three minutes later) Okay, Sandwich staff, it's time to take the order. While your partner orders, you should place check marks on the order form and tell him/her the price. Customers, order your sandwich using the sample dialog.

Ryan's Tip

1. 샌드위치 주문에 필요한 단어는 155쪽의 worksheet을 이용하여 학습할 수 있습니다.

5-7 Order Your Sandwich

(Customer's Order Form)

1. Choose your size
( ) 6 inches - $2.99
( ) Foot long - $3.55

2. Choose your bread
( ) White bread   ( ) Whole wheat bread
( ) Honey oat bread ( ) Chocolate bread

3. Choose your sandwich
( ) Ham & turkey   ( ) Chicken breast
( ) Tuna   ( ) Roast beef
( ) Chicken & bacon ( ) Crab

4. Toasted
( ) Yes   ( ) No

5. Cheese
( ) Yes ($1.00)   ( ) No

6. Choose your vegetable
(Choose as many as you want.)
( ) lettuce ( ) onion   ( ) olive
( ) tomato   ( ) pepper ( ) cucumber

7. Choose your dressing
( ) honey mustard ( ) ranch
( ) vinegar   ( ) mayonnaise

8. Choose your drink
( ) Soda (fountain drink) - $1.00
( ) water (Free)
( ) Combo (Soda + a bag of chips) - $1.50

Total : $ _____

(Sandwich Staff's Order Form)

1. Choose your size
( ) 6 inches - $2.99
( ) Foot long - $3.55

2. Choose your bread
( ) White bread   ( ) Whole wheat bread
( ) Honey oat bread ( ) Chocolate bread

3. Choose your sandwich
( ) Ham & turkey   ( ) Chicken breast
( ) Tuna   ( ) Roast beef
( ) Chicken & bacon ( ) Crab

4. Toasted
( ) Yes   ( ) No

5. Cheese
( ) Yes ($1.00)   ( ) No

6. Choose your vegetable
(Choose as many as you want.)
( ) lettuce ( ) onion   ( ) olive
( ) tomato   ( ) pepper ( ) cucumber

7. Choose your dressing
( ) honey mustard ( ) ranch
( ) vinegar   ( ) mayonnaise

8. Choose your drink
( ) Soda (fountain drink) - $1.00
( ) water (Free)
( ) Combo (Soda + a bag of chips) - $1.50

Total : $ _____

Vocabulary Activities

(Sample Dialog)

- **A** : Hi, what would you like?
- **B** : A foot long wheat bread, roast beef, please.

- **A** : Would you like it toasted?
- **B** : Yes, please.

- **A** : Would you like some cheese?
- **B** : No, thank you.

- **A** : Vegetables?
- **B** : Lettuce, peppers and cucumber.

- **A** : What would you like for dressing?
- **B** : Honey mustard would be good.

- **A** : What would you like for a drink?
- **B** : Combo meal, please.

- **A** : That comes to $.4.05.
- **B** : Thank you so much. Have a good day.

- **A** : You, too.

(Sample Dialog)

- **A** : Hi, what would you like?
- **B** : A foot long wheat bread, roast beef, please.

- **A** : Would you like it toasted?
- **B** : Yes, please.

- **A** : Would you like some cheese?
- **B** : No, thank you.

- **A** : Vegetables?
- **B** : Lettuce, peppers and cucumber.

- **A** : What would you like for dressing?
- **B** : Honey mustard would be good.

- **A** : What would you like for a drink?
- **B** : Combo meal, please.

- **A** : That comes to $.4.05.
- **B** : Thank you so much. Have a good day.

- **A** : You, too.

(Sample Dialog)

- **A** : Hi, what would you like?
- **B** : A foot long wheat bread, roast beef, please.

- **A** : Would you like it toasted?
- **B** : Yes, please.

- **A** : Would you like some cheese?
- **B** : No, thank you.

- **A** : Vegetables?
- **B** : Lettuce, peppers and cucumber.

- **A** : What would you like for dressing?
- **B** : Honey mustard would be good.

- **A** : What would you like for a drink?
- **B** : Combo meal, please.

- **A** : That comes to $.4.05.
- **B** : Thank you so much. Have a good day.

- **A** : You, too.

(Sample Dialog)

- **A** : Hi, what would you like?
- **B** : A foot long wheat bread, roast beef, please.

- **A** : Would you like it toasted?
- **B** : Yes, please.

- **A** : Would you like some cheese?
- **B** : No, thank you.

- **A** : Vegetables?
- **B** : Lettuce, peppers and cucumber.

- **A** : What would you like for dressing?
- **B** : Honey mustard would be good.

- **A** : What would you like for a drink?
- **B** : Combo meal, please.

- **A** : That comes to $.4.05.
- **B** : Thank you so much. Have a good day.

- **A** : You, too.

5-7 Order Your Sandwich

Fill in the blanks with right English words

crab	turkey	chicken breast	toasted	roast beef
mayonnaise	mustard	tuna	whole wheat bread
pepper	cucumber	vinegar	ranch	foot long
oat bread	onion	fountain drink	lettuce

Meaning	Words	Meaning	Words
약 30cm		양상추	
통밀로 만든 빵		양파	
귀리로 만든 빵		피망	
칠면조		오이	
닭가슴살		겨자	
참치		식초	
로스트 비프		마요네즈	
게맛살		랜치 드레싱	
오븐에 살짝 구운		콜라, 사이다 등의 음료	

Fill in the blanks with right English words

crab	turkey	chicken breast	toasted	roast beef
mayonnaise	mustard	tuna	whole wheat bread
pepper	cucumber	vinegar	ranch	foot long
oat bread	onion	fountain drink	lettuce

Meaning	Words	Meaning	Words
약 30cm		양상추	
통밀로 만든 빵		양파	
귀리로 만든 빵		피망	
칠면조		오이	
닭가슴살		겨자	
참치		식초	
로스트 비프		마요네즈	
게맛살		랜치 드레싱	
오븐에 살짝 구운		콜라, 사이다 등의 음료	

Vocabulary Activities

5-8 Vocabulary Quiz Board Game

Type
Group work / Vocabulary

Aim
To test students' vocabulary by playing a board game

Level
All level

Time
30 ~ 40 minutes

Language
Vocabulary Test

How to do the activity

1. 이 활동은 단어 퀴즈에 쓰면 좋습니다. 미리 전 차시에 학생들에게 일정 분량의 단어를 제시하고 암기해 오도록 지시합니다.

2. 4~5명의 학생이 한 모둠을 만듭니다. 게임의 진행자를 한 명 선정합니다. 단어를 잘 외워오지 않았거나 영어에 자신이 없는 학생을 진행자로 선정하는 것이 좋습니다.

3. 진행을 맡은 학생은 157쪽의 보드게임 판을 받습니다. 그리고 오늘 퀴즈를 보게 될 단어를 이용하여 그 모둠 만의 보드게임을 만들도록 합니다. 학생들이 취향대로 보드게임을 만들어도 되지만 기본적인 제작 방식은 다음과 같습니다.

(1) 보드게임 빈 칸에 학생들이 암기해 온 단어를 적절하게 배치합니다. 외워온 단어가 많으면 2개 이상의 단어를 한 칸에 쓰는 것이 좋습니다. "Go to Start" "Go 2 steps back" "Go 2 steps forward" "Bring the leader here" 등의 재미있는 지시사항 칸에는 아무 것도 쓰지 않도록 합니다.

(2) 진행자가 보드게임을 만드는 동안 다른 학생들은 단어를 외울 수 있도록 합니다. 절대 다른 학생들에게 보드게임을 보여 줘서는 안됩니다.

4. 게임의 진행방식은 다음과 같습니다.

(1) 주사위를 던져서 이동합니다. 만일 1, 2가 나오면 1칸, 3, 4가 나오면 2칸, 5, 6이 나오면 3칸을 이동합니다.

(2) 주사위을 던져서 이동한 칸에 있는 단어를 읽고 그 단어의 뜻을 말해야 합니다. 만일 단어의 뜻을 제대로 말하지 못하면 2칸 뒤로 이동합니다. 2칸 뒤로 이동한 뒤에는 다시 단어를 말하거나 그 지시사항을 따르지 않습니다.

(3) 단어의 뜻을 제대로 말했는지 확인하는 것은 보드게임을 만든 사회자의 일입니다.

(4) 단어 이외에 다른 지시사항의 칸에 도착하면 그 지시사항을 따르도록 합니다.

(5) 가장 빨리 Finish 에 도착하는 학생이 승리합니다. 만일 시간 내로 게임을 끝내지 못하면 가장 멀리 이동한 학생이 승리합니다.

Teacher's Talk

1. Today, we're going to play a vocabulary board game. First, make groups of five students and then choose a group leader who will create your team's board game.

2. (After choosing the group leaders) Board game maker, come here so I can explain how to make the board game. The rest of you should study the words.

3. (Explain how to make the board game as well as how to play the game in Korean.)

4. Everyone, put away your books. It's time to play the game.

5-8 Vocabulary Quiz Board Game

Start					Go 2 steps back		

→ **Let's Play English Word Board Game!!!** ↓

Go 2 steps back

	Go 2 steps back		Bring the first player here				

↓

1. 🎲 🎲 = go one step forward
2. 🎲 🎲 = go two steps forward
3. 🎲 🎲 = go three steps forward

↓

Bring the last player here			Go 2 steps back		Change with the first player		

1. If you cannot tell the meaning of the word, you have to go two steps back.
2. Follow the instructions of where you have moved.
3. If you move back two steps back, you don't need to follow the instructions.

←

End	Go to Start						Change with the last player

📺 Vocabulary Activities

5-9 Fix Your Konglish

Type
Group Work / Vocabulary

Aim
To learn about improper English expressions (Konglish)

Level
Beginner ~ pre-intermediate

Time
15 ~ 20 minutes

Language
Improper English expressions (Konglish)

How to do the activity

1. 4명의 학생들이 한 모둠이 되도록 합니다.

2. 159~160쪽에 있는 Real English 카드와 Konglish 카드를 자른 뒤 잘 섞어서 각 모둠에 나누어 줍니다. 각 모둠의 학생들은 협동을 통해서 Real English 카드와 Konglish 카드를 따로 구별해서 분류해야 합니다.

3. 학생들의 활동이 끝나면 교사와 함께 어떤 표현이 Konglish인지, 그 표현을 어떻게 올바르게 사용하는지 학습하도록 합니다.

4. 학습이 끝난 뒤, 161쪽에 있는 만화 worksheet을 나누어 주고 배운 표현을 이용하여 빈 칸을 완성하도록 합니다.

Teacher's Talk

1. Make groups of four students. I'm going to give you two types of cards; one of them is a real English card and the other one is a Konglish card. Within your group, you need to separate the real English cards from the Konglish ones. I'll give you one minute to separate the cards.

2. Good job! Let's check which expressions are real English and which ones are Konglish. Kisu, can you tell us which expressions are real English?

3. Now, I'm going to give you a cartoon. Look at the pictures and then fill in the blanks with the real English expressions that you've just learned. Make sure not to use Konglish. I'll give you 3 minutes.

Ryan's Tip

1. 수업시간에 다룬 Konglish 표현 이외에 잘못 사용되고 있는 Konglish를 조사하는 활동을 과제로 제시하는 것도 좋습니다.

2. 학생들의 영어 작문 과제를 검사하다 보면 공통적으로 잘못 사용하는 표현들을 종종 만날 수 있습니다. 그런 표현들을 모아서 이런 활동을 구성해 보시는 것도 좋을 듯 합니다.

5-9 Fix Your Konglish

(Real English)	(Konglish)
My mom is a great cook.	My mom is a great cooker.
The comedians are so funny.	The comedians are so fun.
Time's up! Put down your pen.	Time is over. Put down your pen.
Listening to music is my hobby.	Hearing music is my hobby.
My legs hurt.	My legs are sick.
I eat fried eggs in the morning.	I eat egg fry in the morning.
I like to hang out with my friends at the mall.	I like to play with my friends at the mall.
Look! There's a bat in the tree.	See! There is a bat in the tree.

Vocabulary Activities

(Real English)	(Konglish)
I like to go to the video arcade.	I like to go to game room.
Do not use your cell phone.	Do not use your hand phone.
I don't like students who ride a motorcycle.	I don't like students who ride an autobi.
He cheated on the exam.	He did cunning on the exam.
I need glue for my art project.	I need bond for my art project.
Use white-out to correct the error.	Use white to correct the error.
Using plastic bags is not good for the environment.	Using vinyls is not good for the environment.
I'm looking for my stapler.	I'm looking for my hotchkiss.

Fill in the blanks with the expressions that you've just learned. Be careful not to use Konglish.

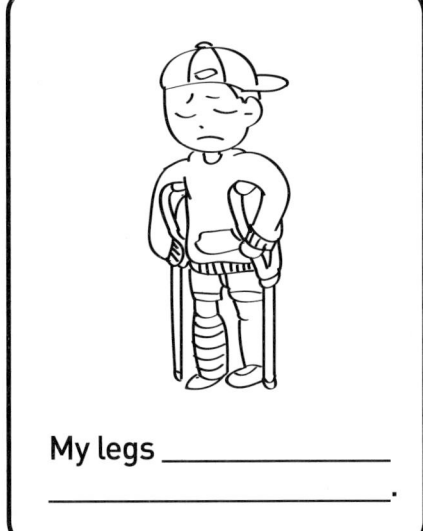

My legs _____ _____.

Don't use your _____ _____.

_____! There's a bat in the tree.

The comedians are so _____.

He _____ on the test.

My mom is a great _____ _____.

I'm looking for my _____.

I don't like students who ride a _____.

_____ is my hobby.

5-10

📺 **Vocabulary Activities**

How Do You Pronounce This Brand?

Type
Solo work / Pronunciation

Aim
To practice proper pronunciations

Level
Beginner ~ pre-intermediate

Time
20 ~ 25 minutes (homework assignment-1 week)

Language
Pronunciation (Phonetic Sounds)

How to do the activity

1. 학생들이 주변에서 흔히 볼 수 있는 영어 브랜드 상표를 불러보도록 합니다. 학생들이 말하는 브랜드를 칠판에 영어로 적습니다.

2. 그 상표들의 제대로 된 영어 발음을 가르쳐 줍니다. 한국말 표기와 비교해서도 가르치고 그 발음이 어떻게 다르게 발음되는지 phonetic sounds를 잠시 설명합니다. 가령 Starbucks가 "스타벅스"로 우리나라 말로 표기되지만 실제 영어 발음은 "스따~ㄹ벅스"에 가깝다는 식으로 설명해 주시면 됩니다. 그리고 "st"가 붙어서 "스ㄸ" 발음으로 되는 다른 단어들의 예도 들어 주시면 됩니다.

3. 학생들에게 164쪽의 worksheet를 나누어 줍니다. 수업시간에 예를 들어 준 것과 동일한 방식으로 우리 주변의 영어 브랜드 상표를 조사하고 그 발음과 관련된 사항을 worksheet의 양식에 맞게 작성하도록 합니다. 일주일 정도의 시간을 주고 과제로 제출하도록 합니다.

4. 일주일 뒤 자신이 작성한 worksheet을 다른 학생들과 공유하도록 합니다.

Teacher's Talk

1. Tell me some common English brand names that you see in Korea. (Eliciting)
2. (Explain the proper pronunciations of the English brand names.)
3. You need to research some common English brand names in Korea. There must be hundreds of names around us. However, choose only 6 words that you think have interesting pronunciations and then complete the worksheet that I'm going to give to you. You should write the brand name or draw the brand logo. Under the brand name or logo, write in Hangul how it is pronounced in Korean and how you should pronounce the word properly. Also, think about other English words that share similar pronunciations.

Ryan's Tip

1. 학생들의 worksheet을 수합하여 Brand Pronunciation Book을 제작하는 것도 재미있는 활동입니다. 이 때는 brand name과 더불어 brand logo를 간단하게 그리도록 하는 것이 좋습니다.

How do you Pronounce This Brand?

(Sample)

Brand name	**Starbucks**	Brand name	**The North Face**
Korean	스타벅스	Korean	노스 페이스
Proper pronunciation	"스트" 가 아니라 "**스ㄸ**" 소리로 됨	Proper pronunciation	"노스"에서 "스"가 아니라 윗니 아랫니 사이에 혀를 넣고 빨리 뺌
Similar words	steak / stick steal / steam	Similar words	south / health stealth / wealth

Brand name	**Sponge Bob**	Brand name	**iphone**
Korean	스폰지 밥	Korean	아이폰
Proper pronunciation	"스프"가 아니라 "**스ㅃ**" 소리로 됨	Proper pronunciation	"프" 소리가 아니라 윗니 아래 아랫입술을 넣고 빨리 빼며 나는 소리
Similar words	sport / speed spin / spoon	Similar words	photo / graph alpha / phantom

Brand name	**Asiana Airline**	Brand name	**Bean Pole**
Korean	아시아나	Korean	빈폴
Proper pronunciation	"아시"가 아니라 "에이쥐"로 발음. "쥐"는 약하게 발음	Proper pronunciation	"빈"은 짧게 하지 않고 길게 "빈~"으로 발음
Similar words	John / gym gene / Jane	Similar words	eat / neat dean / lean

📖 **Vocabulary Activities**

How do you Pronounce This Brand?

Student Name:				Student Number:				Class:

Brand name		Brand name	
Korean		Korean	
Proper pronunciation		Proper pronunciation	
Similar words		Similar words	

Brand name		Brand name	
Korean		Korean	
Proper pronunciation		Proper pronunciation	
Similar words		Similar words	

Brand name		Brand name	
Korean		Korean	
Proper pronunciation		Proper pronunciation	
Similar words		Similar words	

영어 수업 평가서

한 학기동안 (_____) 선생님의 영어 수업에 참여해 주셔서 감사합니다.
선생님의 영어 수업에 대한 여러분의 의견을 듣고 싶습니다. 솔직하게 여러분의 의견을 적어 주세요.

	매우 그렇다	그렇다	보통이다	아니다	매우 아니다
1. 선생님께서 수업을 성실하게 준비하신다고 생각하나요?					
2. 선생님께서 진행하시는 영어 활동(게임 등)이 여러분의 흥미를 불러 일으켰나요?					
3. 선생님께서 이해하기 쉽게 수업을 진행하셨나요?					
4. 선생님의 목소리와 말투, 말하는 속도 등은 여러분이 이해하는데 적절하였나요?					
5. 선생님께서 수업시간에 진행하는 영어 단어 퀴즈가 여러분이 공부하는데 도움이 되었나요?					
6. 선생님의 영어 수업이 여러분의 영어 실력 향상에 도움을 주었다고 생각하나요?					
7. 선생님의 영어 수업을 다른 학생들에게 추천하고 싶은가요?					
8. 선생님의 영어 수업 중 좋은 점 두가지를 구체적으로 써 주세요.	1. 2.				
9. 선생님의 영어 수업 중 개선하였으면 하는 점 두가지를 구체적으로 써 주세요.	1. 2.				
10. 마지막으로 선생님께 꼭 드리고 싶은 말을 적어 주세요.					

여러분과 한 학기를 함께 할 수 있어서 행복했습니다. 방학 잘 보내고 웃는 얼굴로 다시 만나길 바랍니다.

(_____) 선생님